MW00794959

Mad
Bomber
Melville
by Leslie James Pickering

Arissa Media Group
Portland, Oregon

MAD BOMBER MELVILLE
Copyright © 2007 by Leslie James Pickering

Arissa Media Group
P.O. Box 6058
Portland, OR 97228
info@arissamediagroup.com
www.arissamediagroup.com

Printed and bound in the United States of America.

First Edition, 2007.

Library of Congress Control Number: 2007928539

International Standard Book Number (ISBN): 0-9742884-4-6

Cover design by Leslie James Pickering and Matthew Haggett

Printed on 100% recycled, acid-free paper.

Arissa Media Group, LLC was formed in 2003 to assist in building a revolutionary consciousness in the United States of America. For more information, wholesale and bulk requests, catalogue listings, submission guidelines, or media inquiries please contact Arissa Media Group, LLC, P.O. Box 6058, Portland, OR 97228. info@arissamediagroup.com • www.arissamediagroup.com

For Nate Buck, Michael B., and everyone who can't help but show that the struggle is more than just political, it's personal.

CONTENTS

1

SHEER STUPIDITY OR STUBBORNNESS

MAD BOMBER MELVILLE

Tonawanda is a town about twelve miles north of Buffalo, New York. It took its name from the American Indians of the Neuter and Erie, meaning "Swift Waters," because it sat along the Niagara River between Lake Erie and Lake Ontario, just upstream from Niagara Falls. The town was one of a number of working-class communities in the Great Lakes region with a strong shipping and industrial economy.[1]

Sam was born in 1934. His parents, Dorothy and William, had a place in the Bronx but divorced before Sam was old enough to remember his father. Dorothy took Sam and moved from New York City back to her Western New York hometown of about 25,000 people.

Life in Tonawanda wasn't easy. Sam later told stories of his mother prostituting to feed the family, and his younger sister not knowing who her father was. When Sam was about four or five he got a cinder stuck in his left eye and went long enough without medical attention that he lost half his vision.

Sam grew to hate his mother's boyfriends, and by the time he was fifteen he couldn't take it anymore. Dorothy had a boyfriend who did nothing but drink and yell at Sam and his sisters while she worked all day. When Sam reached his breaking point he attacked his mother's boyfriend, kicking him out of their house. Before Dorothy came home Sam was gone too.

Sam quit high school and got a room at the YMCA in Buffalo. He found work stacking bowling pins. The job was late hours and the busses stopped running by the time he was let out. Sam loved walking the seven miles from the bowling alley to the YMCA, down the snow-filled Buffalo streets in the dead of the night singing, reciting poetry and yelling up at the stars.

"I was coming out of some building in Buffalo," Sam remembered, "It might have been a courthouse – when I saw my father at the bottom of a long flight of stairs. I don't know how I realized it was him. I had never seen a picture. But I recognized him as if it was a dream. I think I must have flown to the bottom of those steps."[2]

William had remarried and came looking for Sam and his older sister. He convinced Sam to finish high school in Buffalo then move to the Bronx with his new family on the promise that they would get him singing lessons.

Sam had a unique love for the fine arts of music, poetry and the theater. His favorite novel was <u>Moby Dick</u> and he fantasized about singing in the opera. Moving to New York City with his father was a ticket into the world of his dreams.

Sam dissected his "plans for the future" in a high school paper written in the third-person, "He wants to be a music teacher some day, but his dream seems to be a long way off. He's been discouraged many times but always seems to overcome this, either through sheer stupidity or stubbornness."[3]

Back in high school, Sam joined the glee club and the school orchestra. He failed to meet the standard requirements for graduation but was pushed through anyway with the help of sympathetic teachers who he won over with hard work and charm.

After graduating, Sam moved in with his father in New York City and got his voice lessons. He studied several years as an operatic tenor and was a professional choir singer. He was also trained on the tuba, French horn and folk guitar.

William was into music too... and communism. He joined the Communist Party, worked closely with a number of well-known leftist intellectuals like Paul Robeson and Irving Horowitz, and helped to organize taxi driver unions.

Sam remembered his father driving him through Harlem to show him how the poor were forced to live under capitalism, but his father's politics didn't quite fit. Out the window Sam saw kids playing and having fun in the street. The wealthier neighborhoods were sterile, dead. There had to be another answer.

"He was terribly serious about it," Sam remembered, "but I couldn't see it as he did. To me, those kids playing stickball and running through the streets were having a terrific time. I never wanted to have a lot of money and live in a stuffy duplex on Park Avenue. I couldn't believe that anyone else did either."[4]

When William moved the family to a white middle-class neighborhood on Long Island, Sam rejected his father altogether. To Sam, William was selling-out in fear of the nationwide persecution of communists lead by Senator Joseph McCarthy.

MAD BOMBER MELVILLE

When William died of cancer in early 1968, Sam hadn't seen him in many years.

Sam got married in his early twenties. His bride Ruth, the daughter of a middle-class Jewish family, just graduated with a degree in education. Sam got work in Manhattan by lying that he had a civil engineering degree in job applications. He started off as a draftsman and worked his way up through various jobs to a $14,000 per year position.

Sam had a knack for anything mechanical and enjoyed the work, but hated the companies he worked for. When one employer ordered him to begin work on new offices for Chase Manhattan in the brutal apartheid Union of South Africa, Sam erupted in a fury and walked off the job on the spot. When he went home and broke the news to Ruth she called him a communist.

Ruth pressured Sam to provide a middle-class lifestyle but he was finding it unrewarding and intolerable, and his interests were shifting. Sam lost any drive for materialism and was searching for something more meaningful, less superficial. He left Ruth while she was still pregnant.

They tried to get back together just after their son was born, but their lifestyles had grown too far apart. Sam visited his son every week for the first few years, but the conflict between him and Ruth grew more and more violent until Sam struck Ruth in the heat of an argument. He could never gather the nerve to come back after that.

One day Sam called and his son answered the phone. Sam said, "This is Daddy."

There was an awkward silence until he repeated himself, "This is Daddy."

Finally there came an answer, "No, my Daddy's gone away and he's not coming back."[5]

It hurt Sam so much that he never called again. He kept a photograph of his son in his guitar case, which he took with him everywhere, but Sam's son grew up without his father.

For a while Sam drifted, living off odd jobs and unemployment until he got work teaching plumbing design at a trade school through the winter and spring of 1968.

That's when radical activity around Columbia University caught Sam's interest. He quit his teaching job and began working for an underground newspaper called *The Guardian*, making $50 a week for delivery and handy-work around the office. Sam was approaching his mid-thirties and wasn't a student, but he began attending Peace and Freedom Party rallies and joined the Community Action Committee (C.A.C.).

The C.A.C. was a group of a couple dozen Columbia students, Upper West Side radicals and working-class tenants who were organizing against Columbia University's tenant evictions. Columbia was evicting tenants living in apartments that the university wanted to tear down to build an eight-story gymnasium. It was at a C.A.C. demonstration that Sam was first arrested for refusing to vacate an eviction site. The arrest was featured on the television news, showing Sam walking sternly as the police led him into the paddy wagon.[6]

It was also through the C.A.C. that Sam met Jane Alpert. The group organized a sit-in against the eviction of the St. Marks Arms tenants on West 112th Street. Sam saw Jane reading the newspaper there and made his move. He swapped Jane's copy of the *New York Times* for a current issue of *The Guardian*. They got take-out from a nearby coffee shop and Jane gave Sam a check for a year's subscription of *The Guardian*. She gave Sam her phone number on the back of the check.

Jane was enrolled in a graduate program in journalism at Columbia University. She'd gotten her undergraduate with honors from the prestigious Swarthmore College. Her parents lived in upscale Forest Hills and had high expectations of her, but the more Jane led a straight life the more she envied the students who were protesting the Vietnam War and striking at Columbia.

Jane got a call from Sam a week later asking if he could drop by her apartment. He was there in five minutes wearing the same boots, work shirt and jeans he wore at the sit-in.

Jane never met anyone like Sam before. He was more than six-feet-tall, with a broad chest and shoulders, two different colored eyes, very defined features... and he was a revolutionary.

"This country's about to go through a revolution," he told

her. "I expect it to happen before the decade is over and I intend to be a part of it."[7]

They rapped politics and quickly became lovers. Before long, Jane gave Sam a key to the apartment and he moved in with his guitar, a couple shirts and pairs of jeans, a dictionary, a few volumes of poetry and his copy of <u>Moby Dick</u>. It was all he owned.

In November of 1968, Sam and Jane moved from Jane's Upper West Side apartment to the Lower East Side, where poor Puerto Rican kids would burn the nicest cars on the street. Sam would hang out the apartment window cheering them on, at the same time shaking his head at how unproductive and misdirected he felt their anger was.

Jane dropped out of her graduate program at Columbia University, quit her publishing job with the Oxford University Press, and volunteered long hours at the office of the underground *RAT Subterranean News*.

"That winter the talk around our kitchen table turned increasingly to guerrilla action," Jane remembered. "The argument went like this: if the movement was dying, it was because the movement had never really learned how to fight. We had to stop acting like coddled children, scared off by a few arrests, a couple canisters of tear gas."[8]

Wrapped up in these discussions were Pat Swinton and Dave Hughey, both Jane's age. The four were growing very close.

Pat lived in the Lower East Side, a few blocks from Sam and Jane, and worked for the North American Congress on Latin America, a research organization associated with *The Guardian* and Students for a Democratic Society (a national leftist student organization, better known as S.D.S., that organized for civil rights and against the Vietnam War). She had a three-year-old daughter and a degree in education. Pat's parents worked for the U.S. Government, but were Marxists who raised her to think critically of capitalism and U.S. policy.

Dave was Pat's boyfriend who also lived in the Lower East Side and worked doing layouts for *The Guardian* with Sam. Dave grew up with his Baptist Minister father and spent part of his childhood in Sweden and part in the southern U.S. After quitting college he came to New York City, joined the Committee to Aid the N.L.F. (National Liberation Front of South Vietnam) and hung an N.L.F. flag off the Washington Square Arch.

"I had become convinced that bombings, aimed at property rather than people and accompanied by clearly written communiqués that we would send to the press, were the necessary next step in the evolution of our movement," Jane wrote, "and I had no doubt that the love the four of us felt for one another was enough to sustain us through whatever dangers we would face – which we fully believed might include capture and life imprisonment."[9]

"*The Guardian* had... a 20th anniversary, a huge party, a meeting, that took place at the Fillmore East," remembered Liz Fink, then delivery driver for the paper.

"There was all this competition going down and [Sam] wanted none of it... He was the chief security at the event and the event turned into a nightmare, because it was such a turbulent time.... The various factions were at each other's throats. Bernardine Dohrn was there as a representative of S.D.S., and Tom Hayden, and H. Rap Brown, and there became a fight between Rap's bodyguards and S.D.S. It was pretty heavy, and everybody was at each other's throats, right, I mean it was a scene and a half. I can't tell you what a scene and a half it was. Shortly after that, [Sam] left *The Guardian*. He just walked away one day... because it just wasn't militant enough. It was full of shit. And it *was* full of shit."[10]

Back in 1961, Sam's natural tendency to disobey senseless authority got him a $50 fine when he was cited for refusing to take cover during an air-raid drill.[11]

The first time Sam ever went to a protest, police were raiding a student strike at Columbia University. Sam tried to convince the students to fight back and started dragging 50-gallon garbage cans to the roof of the Low Library to hurl onto the police below. He tried to get the students to join him, but they only scattered in fear and confusion. Police grabbed Sam in the act, dragged him into a building, clubbed him and left him tied to a chair. Sam could never understand why nobody would fight back.

The movement wasn't moving enough for Sam, and he wanted to give it a push, so he took to graffiti. He started writing "George Metesky Was Here" on the sides of buildings across New York City.

George Metesky was committed to the Matteawan Asylum for the Criminally Insane after he admitted to planting dozens of pipe bombs around New York City from 1940 to 1956. When Metesky's bombs weren't duds, they usually erupted in public places, like movie theaters and library telephone booths, injuring a number of innocent people and leaving investigators at a loss. His enemy was his former employer and energy giant, Consolidated Edison. Metesky credited his tuberculosis to an injury he got on the job at Consolidated Edison that the company refused to compensate him for.

Metesky's first bomb was found on a windowsill of a Consolidated Edison building with a handwritten note attached, reading, "Con Edison crooks, this is for you." Later notes, written in cut out letters from newspapers and magazines, were mailed threatening, "I will make Con Edison sorry. I will bring them before the bar of Justice – public opinion will condemn them…" and, "…I will bring the Con Edison to justice – they will pay for their dastardly deeds."

The notes were signed "F.P." (standing for "Fair Play") but most knew of Metesky by a nickname the press gave him, "The Mad Bomber."[12]

Sam found inspiration in the way Metesky was able to wage a one-man-war against a large and powerful corporation. With his graffiti, Sam was sending a reminder of the strength of even just one person against the rich and powerful.

Up in Montréal, a group of French-Canadian revolutionaries called the Front de la Liberation de Québec (F.L.Q.) were planting bombs too.

The F.L.Q. was founded by Pierre Vallières, a French-Canadian from the working-class slums of Montréal's East

8

End and the shantytowns of the South Shore. Vallières went underground in 1966 to fight for Québec to become a socialist nation independent from Canada.

In May of 1966, the F.L.Q. bombed the La Grenade shoe factory that had fired all their workers and hired scabs after an eighteen-month strike. The explosion killed one person and injured several others. When Vallières and another F.L.Q. member, Charles Gagnon, went to the United Nations asking for political asylum in France they were arrested for the La Grenade bombing instead. Vallières published a book that he wrote while behind bars called <u>White Niggers of America</u>. The book served as the battle cry for the independence of Québec.[13]

Since the early nineteen sixties, the F.L.Q. had carried out hundreds of guerrilla attacks in Québec, and the arrests of Vallières and Gagnon only seemed to fuel the fire.

On February 13, 1969, a cell of the F.L.Q. set off an explosion that blew out the northeast wall of the Montréal Stock Exchange and seriously injured thirty-eight people. In response, Canadian authorities issued warrants for the arrest of Pierre-Paul Geoffroy, Raymond Villeneuve and Mario Bachand. Pierre-Paul Geoffroy was captured and claimed sole responsibility for a series of bombings so his comrades could evade capture.[14]

Villeneuve and Bachand became fugitives and made a hasty escape from Canada, relying on a single contact in New York City who they were referred to by somebody they'd never met. Only one of them could speak English, barely. When they got to New York City they called their contact from a pay phone, only to find out that the contact wanted nothing to do with them. They were passed from person to person and it seemed nobody in the movement was willing to risk helping them, until Sam's name was brought up.

When Sam got the call he took the two fugitives into his own apartment. Soon a second apartment was secured that belonged to some of Pat's friends who were out of town for a few months.

All of Sam's time went to caring for the F.L.Q. fugitives. He was captivated by their adventure. Dynamite, bomb plots, disguises, hideouts, communiqués, narrow escapes, and revolutionaries on the lam fascinated him.

Every morning Sam went to the Post Office to check if any mail arrived for them from Québec. He bought them clothes, gave them money and did their grocery shopping. He drew up maps of the parts of town where they could stretch their legs without drawing attention. At three o'clock each afternoon, Sam went to the foreign newsstand in Times Square to buy them copies of the Montréal newspapers.

Whenever Sam had a chance he would drill the fugitives on the specifics of wiring dynamite bombs. He took notes and drew up diagrams. They would stay up late into the night going over details of hiding bombs in briefcases, covertly planting them in buildings, safely storing and transporting dynamite, and putting a cloth over the telephone receiver to disguise your voice while making a warning call.

The fugitives were more interested in explaining the political situation in Québec, "If we win independence before we make Marxist revolution, then Québec becomes… a colony of the United States. We do not want to trade government by Toronto for government by Washington. We want to make a communist state independent of both."[15]

The Canadian fugitives weren't sure whether the type of guerrilla warfare the F.L.Q. was waging in Québec should be applied in the U.S., but Sam was.

The Montréal papers from April 2, 1969 told of Pierre-Paul Geoffroy raising a clenched fist to a courtroom of supporters as he was led to prison to serve 124 concurrent life sentences. The fugitives knew there was no going back.

Sam kept trying to come up with false identification for the two from either Canada or France. He made at least two trips up to Québec to meet with F.L.Q. supporters, but still had no luck. The fugitives wanted desperately to be safe under the protection of Cuban leader Fidel Castro. Castro was allowing hijacked planes from the U.S. safe harbor at Cuban airports. Finally, a desperate plan was plotted to hijack a plane and redirect it to Cuba.

Jane went to the library to research the success rates of similar hijackings. She found that their chances looked good. The airlines' main defense was public relations psychology. By cooperating with the media, the Federal Aviation Administration got heavy coverage for failed hijackings and development of security equipment, and reduced coverage of successful hijackings. They also posted signs warning of the penalties of air piracy and offered $25,000 rewards for information leading to the arrest of hijackers. This way, they were able to reduce hijacking by creating the public perception that it had become very risky without running the high costs of searching every passenger, getting high-tech security equipment or lobbying for increased legislation.

Jane found out that only one airline was experimenting with metal detectors and the chances of a successful hijacking were as good as ever. She was so excited about her discoveries that she wrote an unsigned article in the *RAT Subterranean News* about it.[16]

Sam hung out at the airport to observe the boarding of Miami-bound flights, finding that Atlantic Airlines flights were pretty empty and were the most laidback when it came to searching their passengers. Miami-bound flights required the least rerouting and would have enough fuel to make the trip to Cuba. He figured the fewer people on the flight, the lesser the chances of a vigilante passenger attempting to stop the hijacking.

Using a false name over the phone, Jane made two reservations for Atlantic flight 301 leaving from La Guardia on Monday, May 4, 1969. She gave the fugitives $300 for their tickets from her savings. Sam got them a small pistol with a leg holster and a seven-inch hunting knife. They set up chairs in their apartment to simulate airline seating and practiced their hijacking routine. They rehearsed their lines in broken English.

On the day of the flight Sam and Jane discretely saw them off at the airport and went home to watch for news of the hijacking.

"Atlantic Airlines Flight Number 301 from New York to Miami has been diverted to Cuba, where it has now landed," the *Associated Press* reported, "The plane carried seventy-five passengers. It changed course about forty miles from Miami, with no word to ground controls. This is the twenty-fourth hijacking since January 1, 1969."[17]

EXPLO

Explo Industries was the only place in New York City that distributed dynamite. They were granted a citywide monopoly as a means of controlling the explosive and each stick was accounted for by a serial number on the casing. Explo would drop the sticks off at each site at around six in the morning and pick up what was left each evening to keep overnight for safe storage.

Sam learned about Explo by following their trucks to and from blasting sites and looking up "explosives" in the phone book.[1] It would have been nearly risk-free to get dynamite out in rural areas by buying it without identification or stealing it from an unguarded blasting site at night, but Sam wasn't known for being cautious.

The Explo yard was a half-acre compound with two concrete blockhouses surrounded by a high fence, in a mostly deserted industrial section of the Bronx. At night, it was kept guard by an older man and two dogs. One night, the guard found the first dog poisoned, and the next night the second dog disappeared.

On July 7th, 1969, Sam and two young white men put red bandannas over their faces, jumped the fence and stormed into the Explo office. Sam pointed a pistol at the guard and said, "We want dynamite."

The guard didn't resist. They grabbed as much as they could carry and when they asked about detonators, the guard actually told them that the dynamite could be set off with just the blasting caps and an electrical current.

The guard told police that he didn't get the feeling that the robbers wanted to harm him, as long as he cooperated. The police took note that the three were wearing denim work clothes and red bandannas over their faces, instead of the usual combination of sunglasses and a hat, or a ski mask, to hide their identities. It was the only robbery of its kind at the time and investigators were puzzled over why anyone would take such an unnecessary risk to get dynamite, but there were no leads in the case.[2]

Police counted three missing boxes of DuPont dynamite, each containing 65 sticks, and two, fifty-count boxes of blasting caps, totaling 195 sticks of dynamite and 100 blasting caps.[3] Jane Alpert only recalls storing 150 sticks and 50 caps in their apartment.[4] It was alleged by police that *Le Petit Journal*, an underground newspaper from Quebec, claimed that two

Canadians pulled off the robbery with Sam and stole a total of 400 sticks of dynamite.[5] They said the journal claimed that the dynamite was split between the Canadians and Sam and a portion was given to The Black Panther Party, which could account for the missing explosives. But the Panthers never blew anything up and dynamite was much easier to get in Canada than it was in the Bronx. However you look at it, it was a lot of dynamite to be in the hands of a group of revolutionaries ready to do some damage to Manhattan.

The three burst into the apartment where Jane and some others were waiting, nervous and anxious. They carefully set the boxes of explosives down in the middle of the kitchen floor. In the air was a mixture of excitement and fear. They hadn't planned ahead for what to do next. They figured the only place cool enough to keep the summer heat from setting off the dynamite was Sam and Jane's refrigerator.

They formed a secret group of everyone in the room to decide what to use the dynamite on. The group was a collective, where everyone had equal say and decisions were made through a consensus process, but most of the first meeting was wasted on petty debates and disguised efforts to delay putting the explosives to use. Sam was already exhausted with the long-winded meetings that were common in the movement. When it came to dynamite, he wanted action. To him and Jane, it looked like the others were afraid. Sam was trying to improve his patience when it came to working with other people, realizing that revolution was not going to happen overnight, but he spent most of that first meeting leaning against the wall in disgust. The only progress they made was deciding to find somewhere besides Sam and Jane's refrigerator to store the dynamite.

Sam rented a rundown apartment for $60 a month at 67 E. 2nd St. with false identification in the name of "David McCurdy." McCurdy was someone born near Sam's birthday that Jane discovered in a newspaper birth announcement in the archives of the public library. She also found one of a woman her age. The birth announcements listed the hospitals where they were born and the full names of their parents, which was all the information they needed to get copies of birth certificates mailed to them. Jane had hers mailed to the address of a friend from college, to cover her tracks, but Sam wasn't as careful and had his mailed to Pat Swinton's apartment.

Once the dynamite was moved in, he spent at least a few hours each day at "McCurdy's Place," to keep the landlord from getting suspicious and to practice wiring up timing devices. Nobody else from the collective was interested in helping to care for the dynamite, so Sam took the liberty of giving a spare set of keys to Dave Hughey who had just quit his job at *The Guardian* and lived only a block away from McCurdy's Place.

Jane wanted Dave and Pat in the collective, but at their first meeting the others voted against it. Jane had been talking with Sam, Pat and Dave since the winter about forming their own guerrilla group, but now she felt responsibility towards a collective of people she hardly knew.

Sam seemed to regard the collective as only one of a number of ways that the dynamite could be used. The Explo robbery was his idea and at the last minute the other two got nervous and Sam had to threaten to go ahead alone to keep them from turning back. He didn't commit a robbery just to see dynamite sit in his refrigerator while he sat around talking about the upcoming Woodstock Music and Art Festival. The stuff was going to be used.[6]

United Fruit Pier Bombed

New York (LNS) – A pier on the Hudson River owned by the United Fruit Company was blasted by a bomb on midnight of Cuban Independence Day, July 26th. Police said the bomb was either dynamite or a plastic explosive and that they were investigating the "motives and method."

An anonymous caller verified that the explosion, which blew a hole in the guard-patrolled pier and tore up a shipping crate and part of a door, injuring no one, was in "celebration of Cuban Independence Day."

EXPLO

This was at least the second act of apparently political sabotage in the New York/ New Jersey area in a month. Earlier in July, a military grenade arsenal burst into flames as a result of either deliberate arson or a planted bomb. The arsenal was used to store a variety of demolition equipment for use by the U.S. Army.

The United Fruit Company is one of the largest American Capitalists in Latin America. It owned a large part of Cuba before the Revolution, and it has large holdings today in Venezuela, Peru, Columbia and other Latin American Countries.[7]

At that time, a number of active piers still jutted out into the mouth of the Hudson River from Manhattan. Sam had been watching the pier long enough to know it was deserted after six every evening. Sam came to Jane for help with the bombing and suggested they just ask Pat to come along instead of involving the collective. The three met at eight p.m. and Sam assembled two bombs from 40 sticks of dynamite, blasting caps and wind-up alarm clocks and placed them inside vinyl pocketbooks. They then went down to the pier, where Sam planted the bombs against a set of large steel doors while Jane and Pat kept watch.[8]

In 1969, the United Fruit Company was well known for its role in Latin America, having grown to be the biggest name in Latin American imperialism by monopolizing arable land in the region. They owned so much land in Latin America that many peasants lived their whole lives without ever leaving United Fruit property. Outside of their extensive food product operations, the company owned 900 miles of Latin American railways, the Tropical Radio Telegraph Co., Swiss Chalet restaurants and hotels, 3,000 A&W Drive-ins, and over 600 Baskin-Robbins ice cream parlors. In 1969 alone, United Fruit had revenues of $509.5 million. Thirteen of United Fruit's eighteen ships were under charter to the U.S. Navy in 1969, bringing supplies to Southeast Asia.[9] Sam, Jane and Pat figured an attack against United Fruit was sure to gain support within the movement.

The three were shocked at how simple it was. The area

17

around the pier was pretty much abandoned at that hour, so there was nobody around to witness. It really wasn't much harder than delivering a package, and they were anxious to read all about it on tomorrow's front page. Sam was sure that once the collective saw how easy and safe it was, they wouldn't hesitate to use the dynamite the next time around.

On their way home the three joked about how stupid it was of United Fruit to have the company's name spelled out in large letters across the top of the building to be seen from miles away. If the company didn't have such a big ego the pier probably would never have been bombed. What the bombers didn't know was that United Fruit had changed the location of their New York City shipments of Chiquita bananas and were leasing the old pier out to a tugboat operator who had nothing to do with imperialism in Latin America.

They scanned the radio that evening and the papers the next day but couldn't find a word on the bombing. The third day Sam called in an anonymous tip from a payphone with a handkerchief over the receiver to W.B.A.I. The liberal radio station gave a brief report on the bombing and Jane wrote a short article for the next issue of *RAT Subterranean News* as though she had only known about the bombing from the radio.[10]

Behind the large steel doors, where the bombs were placed, sat a shipment of thirty tons of peat-moss planters. While the door and part of the dock were destroyed, most of the shock from the explosion was absorbed between the peat and the Hudson River.[11]

Barely making the news, causing only minor damage, and with United Fruit not even occupying the pier, the attack was pretty much a failure. What really bothered Sam, though, was how much dynamite they wasted. Forty sticks was roughly a quarter of their supply, and it had only been nineteen days since the Explo robbery. At that rate the rest of the dynamite would be gone in a couple of months and nobody would know the difference. Sam told himself that next time he wouldn't just leave the dynamite outside a building, he'd put it somewhere it would really cause damage.

The old United Fruit pier wasn't the first place hit by

the Explo dynamite. On July 12, 1969, just five days after the Explo robbery, a series of blasts ripped apart a munitions plant in Washington, New Jersey. The plant was owned by Pyronics, Inc., and produced grenades without metal casings for military training purposes. The explosion shook rural Warren County and could be seen from 20 miles away.[12]

It appears that Sam chose this rural munitions plant as a bomb-testing site. It was a safe enough location and he wouldn't shed a tear over blowing it up, but it got almost no media coverage, had no communiqué, and was never resolved in court.

Surprisingly, the loss of dynamite at United Fruit didn't seem to concern the rest of the collective. If anything, it actually helped to put them at ease. They were much more upset about the bombing taking place without their knowledge. Sam was surprised to hear that they thought he was acting recklessly by involving Pat in the bombing and using the dynamite without first consulting the collective. They even thought the term "Cuban Independence Day" sounded too right wing. After airing their concerns, the collective postponed meeting for the next couple of weeks. Until then they didn't plan on having time for anything but the Woodstock music festival. Sam couldn't have cared less about Woodstock.[13]

On August 20th, 1969, Sam wired up some dynamite and took a stroll through lower Manhattan. He set the timer before he left, not even knowing where he was going to plant the bomb. He decided on the Marine Midland Bank building at 140 Broadway, a 52-story glass skyscraper owned by W.R. Grace & Co.

"I just walked around Wall Street until I found a likely-looking place." Jane recalled Sam explaining, "It's one of those big new skyscrapers, millions of dollars of glass and steel, some fucking phony sculpture in the front. You just look at the building and the people going in and out of it, and you know."[14]

The Marine Midland building, now owned by HSBC Bank, was only two years old at the time and featured a large modern sculpture at its front entrance by Isamu Noguchi, which is basically a brightly colored cube with a hole through it.

A witness to the explosion called it "a nightmare... There

was a deafening roar and the whole building seemed to be falling down."[15]

The bomb exploded near one of the elevator shafts on the eighth floor at eleven that night. It caused severe damage to the building, especially the seventh and eighth floors, which were occupied by about 150 employees of the Marine Midland Grace Trust when the bomb went off. Sixteen late-shift clerical workers and one patrolman suffered shock, cuts and bruises.[16]

The *New York Post* reported, "The blast knocked out several banks of elevators, shut off electricity to the floor for twelve hours, shattered windows and ripped out sections of the tiled ceiling. Files were overturned by the explosion and their contents singed. A section of the ceiling was also ripped out on the seventh floor... A hole 8 by 10 feet was blown in the floor in front of the elevator. The shock tore down the eighth-floor ceiling and ripped an 18-foot crevasse in the floor, sending debris showering to the seventh floor. Broken plaster covered almost everything with fine dust; metal partitions were blown down or shattered; steel girders, some bent, were exposed behind the blasted walls, and cracks were visible in the elevator shaft. Eight of the building's elevators, which service the building's first 27 floors, were put out of commission."[17]

From the street you could see the windows blown out on the seventh and eighth floors on three sides of the building and the plaza below was showered with shards of glass, shreds of paper and other debris.[18] The blast pushed a two-ton computer three feet out of place.[19]

The N.Y.P.D. bomb squad estimated that 20-25 sticks of dynamite were used in the job.[20] They told the *New York Post*, "It looks like the job of a demolition expert."

Jane said she came home and learned about the bomb shortly before it went off. She convinced Sam, she wrote, to go with her to place a warning call, and that when she called, she wasn't taken seriously because she had a woman's voice.

To Jane, Sam's recklessness in the Marine Midland bombing was a sign that he should not be left to work alone. By her account, Sam had no intention of placing a warning call, and knew nothing more about Marine Midland than what he could gather from a glance at their building. [21]

Unlike United Fruit, Marine Midland was relatively unknown in the movement, even though Marine Midland Grace Trust ranked as America's 19th largest bank, W.R. Grace & Co. placed 45th in Fortune's 1968 ranking of industrial corporations, and owner J. Peter Grace Jr. himself was worth $8.9 million. The company's holdings were very diverse, ranging from chemical to food, oil, textiles, transportation and advertising. Grace's grandfather was the first Catholic Mayor of New York City, and in 1879 he got a contract to sell munitions and ships to Peru for its war with Chile. By the end of the war, Peru owed $250 million, which meant Grace virtually owned the country.[22]

Jane had never even heard of Marine Midland before. It was only because Pat came up with some quick research on the company through her work with the North American Congress on Latin America that they were able to put some relevant politics behind the bombing.

Wall Street Bombing

Pictures of Che Guevara adorn the walls of many a hip home and growing numbers are on to the fact that U.S. Business spends an enormous portion of its time raping the third world. Everyone can reel off names of a few hungry imperialist giants. There's United Fruit, there's Standard Oil, there's Chase Manhattan, there's...

If you lived in Latin America, you could reel off a lot more names. And one of them you wouldn't leave out is W.R. Grace Co. The empire of Peter Grace (which includes, as the banking division, Marine Midland Grace Trust) is hard to ignore. Grace owns land, shipping facilities, chemical plants, economies and people.

The empire got its start in bird shit. Don't laugh, it's profitable business. Bird Shit (guano) is "harvested" off islands in the Pacific and used as fertilizer. But, Grace quickly moved into more dignified pursuits. Grace became The name in Latin American shipping... and also owned an airline (Panagra) until recently. It now has extensive interests in sugar – Grace sugar plantations were just nationalized in Peru – and has complementary interests in a variety of products which are sugar derivatives, like liquor and chemicals. The company's current trend is to diversify itself out of land holdings (which aren't the safest investments during times of nationalistic fervor) and into concerns like chemicals.

There are reasons why Grace isn't known as a household word. U.S. Business is, after all, an elite operation, and people aren't raised to think that business is the sort of thing they should try to understand; it's a given. Grace is just a name on another office building. But for Latin Americans, Grace – W.R. Grace, Marine Midland Grace – is an enemy, an owner. That, apparently, is why Marine Midland Bank was bombed.[23]

"The effect of the actual injuries on [Sam] was profound." Jane wrote, "He was so badly shaken by the unintentional results of the Marine Midland bombing that his disgust with the collective turned into a desperation that it survive. He seemed to realize for the first time that a collective was not just a practical aid but a very real political need. As long as he acted in isolation he was in danger of losing his political vision... He had a vision that his anger could be much more than that, and that with the help of other people he could turn it in a direction that could move others to action and hence become part of a social revolution. But only with the help of other people."[24]

How no one was seriously hurt in such a reckless attack is something between chance and a miracle. That the collective stayed together after the Marine Midland bombing is also surprising. It was a combination of sympathy for Sam and guilt for their own inaction that motivated them to stay up late drafting a communiqué for the attack in a desperate attempt to rationalize the outburst.

Jane took a lead role in keeping the collective together and active from then on. She got everyone to agree to an action before another month passed. If not, they would disband and dispose of the dynamite. She typed and mailed the final copies of the Marine Midland communiqué to *RAT Subterranean News*, *The Guardian* and the *Liberation News Service* (LNS), a radical newswire service.[25]

THIS RELEASE IS FOR THE
UNDERGROUND MEDIA ONLY
THERE WILL BE NO COMMUNICATION
WITH THE PIG MEDIA

The explosive device set off at the Marine Midland Grace Trust Company on the night of August 20th was an act of political sabotage. Considerable damage was done to the security files and building structure of the W.R. Grace Company which extensively controls agricultural and chemical holdings throughout Latin America.

There was no intent to hurt anyone. The attack was directed only at property. An hour before the explosion a W.R. Grace guard was telephoned and advised to clear the building at 140 Broadway. Were this warning not treated as a hoax, the minor injuries sustained by 17 people would have been avoided.

This was the third of such acts, beginning with the explosion of a grenade arsenal in New Jersey on July 15 and the blowing up of a United Fruit pier on July 26, commemorating the Cuban Revolution.

Crimes against other peoples of the world are every bit as heinous as crimes against Americans. Jailing and killing will not detour acts of sabotage in the U.S.; nor will the age-old

political placebo known as "liberal reform." Nor
will the longed for ending of the war in Vietnam
even begin to end the war in the U.S. Nor in
short is there anything the government can do
to placate the impulse to revolution that is in the
blood of young America from coast to coast.[26]

Their work paid off. Articles appeared in underground newspapers
across the country and the bombing gained support, regardless of
the minor injuries and the fact that Marine Midland Grace meant
nothing to the movement the day before.

Jane was working at *RAT Subterranean News* when the
editor opened the communiqué and yelled, "Far fucking out!" She
discretely smiled to herself as he read the words she'd typed the
night before out loud to everyone in the office. [27]

VIETNAM IN MANHATTAN 3

MAD BOMBER MELVILLE

It's 1969. The Vietnam War has been raging for years and the news flashes images of the carnage while tallying the mounting death tolls. The kids you knew that signed up back in '65 either come home dead or something maybe even worse than dead. It seems that every day you hear about friends getting called down for their physicals, and you're stressing over tomorrow's mail.

The whole atmosphere in America has changed in the last few years. Protest, dissent and resistance are everywhere now. The opposition to the war has grown so much it's taken for granted. Even the Beatles have gone from writing songs about having nothing but love eight days a week to singing about people who say they want a revolution. The cultural gap between American youth and the people in government who are drafting them off to be killed has widened so much that the kids relate more to the Viet Cong.

It's not hard to imagine why so many young Americans were against the war in Vietnam. It was killing them. A movement against the war could save their lives. The biggest threat to American youth was their own government. If you hadn't progressed from being against the war to being a revolutionary, you were a liberal. If you weren't itching for something bigger than another protest, you weren't down.

Jane put it in context saying, "The continuing involvement of the United States in the Vietnam War remained the essential condition for all our bombings. Nixon, since taking office in January 1969, had reneged on virtually every promise he made in the campaign. He produced no 'Secret Plan' for peace; he had widened rather than called a halt to the war; and instead of withdrawing troops, he had instituted the paper-stuffing tactic of lowering troop ceilings. Photographs of children on fire from American napalm and adults shot down in cold blood by American soldiers had become part of the steady diet of news programs and part of our political assumptions as well. While public opinion polls showed that a majority of Americans opposed the war, reports of atrocities multiplied – all of them officially denied by the administration. We in the radical left believed that we were facing a situation similar to that which had prevailed in Nazi Germany. If we could only manage to interfere materially with the work of the U.S. Army, we believed we would have widespread support, and the destruction we caused would be its own justification."[1]

> As Richard Nixon was talking "peace" at the U.N. on Thursday, Sept. 18, and his masters of war were relentlessly dealing out death and destruction throughout the world, a time bomb was placed in the Federal Building at 26 Federal Plaza.
>
> The specific targets of this action were the Dept. of the Army, located on the 40th floor (which also houses the Dept. of Commerce) and the Selective Service System, located directly below the Army office.
>
> As in previous bombings, a warning was phoned to the building's security number, the police bomb squad and the police emergency number in ample time to clear the building. Although the police bomb squad did not respond, there were no injuries to personnel when the bomb exploded on schedule at 2 a.m..
>
> This was an act of solidarity with our brother and sister revolutionaries all over the world and with black and brown communities in this country who are fighting to rid the world of American domination and exploitation.[2]

Forget about Marine Midland. The Federal Building at Foley Square in Manhattan was the tallest federal structure in the United States, and second in square footage only to the Pentagon.[3] The explosion destroyed the offices of the U.S. Army that was fighting the ground war in Vietnam, and the Selective Service that was drafting young Americans into the war. This time there would be no questions about the motive, because the bomb spoke for itself.

To prevent the kind of injuries that happened at the 10:47

p.m. Marine Midland explosion, the Federal Building timer was set to detonate at two in the morning. But to repeat the amount of damage, the bomb was placed in a transformer room near a bank of elevators and the men's room, where water lines ran. The communiqué was done smarter too. It was sent out directly to the major media, and it was in the mail early so it would arrive when news of the explosion was still hot on the presses. The papers reported the damages in detail.

"The north end of the 40th floor was covered with debris," wrote the *New York Times*. "A six-foot-square hole had been ripped in a wall opposite the shaftway that contained circuit breakers, electric panels, ducts and utility wires. File cabinets and furniture had been smashed by flying pieces of concrete. A 25-by-40-foot section of the ceiling had been ripped out and the floor on the 41st floor was damaged. Ceiling tiles fell onto the floor, desks and files of the selective service offices that are on the 39th floor of the Federal Office building... the 41-story building, housing some 60 Federal agencies, was closed yesterday to the general public and to most of the 6,000 employees... All water and electrical systems were out of order. A New York Telephone Company spokesman said 4,000 telephones had been rendered inoperable."[4]

The *New York Post* said, "the explosion occurred in a 10-by-12-foot utility shaft on the 40th floor... the blast broke a five-inch water pipe which flooded much of the northeast section of the building, severed electrical wiring, phone lines and gas pipes, and halted elevator service to many of the floors... Water damage was evident as far down as the 27th floor, but some minor damage was reported as low as the 2nd floor. The building was closed to the 6,000 workers [due to the] 'non-safe' condition in the building, no fire protection because of the broken water pipe, no air conditioning, no elevators and weakened floors in the blast area."[5]

According to Jane's memoirs,[6] the Federal Building bombing was the collective's first action. It was planned and executed by the group, dividing the duties of casing the building, wiring the dynamite, planting the bomb, calling in the warnings, and writing, typing and mailing the communiqué between the members.

VIETNAM IN MANHATTAN

In the presence of all of us Sam assembled a bomb from a Westclox wind-up alarm clock, a blasting cap and fifteen sticks of dynamite he'd brought over earlier from the McCurdy apartment. He placed the device in a large purse I had stolen from a midtown department store. Carefully I slid the strap over my right shoulder. The other five wished me luck. I felt very solemn, acutely conscious that I might never come back home. I saluted them and left...

I boarded a bus heading downtown. I was wearing a white A-line dress, kid gloves (to avoid leaving fingerprints), and a touch of make-up. I looked as if I were going to a business lunch or a matinee. I felt as I imagined I would on my wedding day, if I ever married. A kind of agitation coursed through my body, heightening all my faculties. I cushioned my purse on my lap, protecting it from the bus's sudden jolts...

I got off at Foley Square and walked to 26 Federal Plaza. The Federal Building, some sixty stories of tinted glass and steel, dominated the landscape at the foot of Foley Square. Sam and I had sat outside the building every night for the past week, watching until the last light went out on the thirty-ninth and fortieth floors. Near quitting time on this Thursday afternoon, the lobby bustled with civil servants, secretaries, managers, clerks, maintenance men and women. Tonight at 2:00 A.M., when the bomb exploded, the halls would be dark and deserted, the people who worked here safe in their beds – or so we hoped. I found the right bank of elevators and rode up to the fortieth floor, occupied entirely by the department of the Army...

I made sure no one was around before I opened the door. I found a space for the purse behind a bulky piece of machinery, pushed the straps out of sight, and closed the door behind me as I left. I rode the elevator down to the lobby alone and emerged again into the swirling crowd. A guard stared at me as I went out the glass doors. Had he noticed that I came in with a pocketbook and left without one? I turned my head to avoid giving him a good look at my face.[7]

An hour before the bomb was due to explode, the collective regrouped on the roof of an apartment building with a telescope focused on Foley Square. The clock ticked down to the moment when they would be hunted by the government and idolized by the movement. They watched in awe as, at two a.m., the lights on the Federal Building all went black.

"In a moment everyone was talking at once," Jane remembered. "I didn't know what the other five were feeling, but at that moment my joy was undiluted. I had shown Sam he didn't have to act alone; I had caused real injury to the work of the U.S. Army; and I had, perhaps, brought revolution an inch or two closer. An hour later the radio news confirmed our success. The explosive had been massive but had injured no one. For a few hours that night I wanted no more happiness."[8]

Destruction of federal property brought federal investigation. Up until that point the bombings fell mainly under the jurisdiction of the New York Police Department. Now the Federal Bureau of Investigation, with all its resources, was on the case. The F.B.I. tried to question Sam and Jane at an old address the day after the Federal Building bombing. Once the F.B.I. left, the new tenants gave them a heads-up.[9]

After N.Y.P.D. detectives discovered that the *RAT Subterranean News* received a communiqué for the Marine Midland bombing, they paid a visit to their offices. The place was a mess. A neon sign out front of the building that once read, "PHOTOGRAPHS WHILE YOU WAIT" was altered to read "**HOT** RAT*S WHILE YOU WAIT." It was nothing like police headquarters downtown.

VIETNAM IN MANHATTAN

They asked for the original communiqué but Jane, who was in the office, told detectives that it went out with the trash. Before they left they picked up four months of back issues of the underground paper to take back to the station. [10] On page 6 of the August 12-26, 1969 issue they found what they took as an exclusive story on the United Fruit bombing. It was good enough to get a judge to grant a search warrant.

On September 24th, the N.Y.P.D. raided the *RAT* office and found a draft of the United Fruit story that had edits done in pencil.[11] When they asked who would've usually opened the mail the morning the Marine Midland communiqué came, an assistant editor said, "Jane Alpert."[12]

Meanwhile, the bomb squad was gathering evidence. Out of the ashes of Marine Midland they uncovered a mainspring from a Westclox "Baby Ben," the most common hand-wound clock in America.[13] They would find another at the Federal Building.[14]

It looked like the authorities had just about everything they needed to solve the case, but they were far from it. The F.B.I. and the N.Y.P.D. weren't very good at coordinating and sharing information to make busts. While the N.Y.P.D. had a strong suspicion that *RAT* was somehow connected to the bombings, that connection could have been one of potentially hundreds of people that made their way through the *RAT* office. The F.B.I. had only stopped by Sam's old apartment suspecting that he might know something about the F.L.Q. fugitives. Sam had been stopped at the Canadian border a couple times and drew the attention of Canadian authorities, who asked the F.B.I. to check him out for them. They had no suspicion that he robbed the Explo dynamite and was behind the bombings of the Pyronics munitions plant, United Fruit pier, the Marine Midland tower, and now the Federal Building.[15]

The U.S. Army Induction Center was housed in a fancy building on Whitehall Street, erected in 1881. On the ground floor a large sign read, "THE SECURITY OF THE WORLD STARTS HERE."[16]

Whitehall was where all the draft-eligible males in Manhattan reported to take their physicals and be inducted into the Army. It was also where the Selective Service records of thousands of draft-eligible men were kept. The loss of these records would immobilize the draft locally.[17]

The Induction Center was a clear target for the movement against the Vietnam War. Massive protests were held in front of the building for several days in late 1967. In 1968, the mother of a young man killed in Vietnam, along with two other women and five men, chained herself to a 26 year old who was called for induction there.[18]

On October 7, 1969, at 11:25 p.m., an explosion erupted in the fifth floor women's room.

"That night the Whitehall Induction Center was virtually leveled," Jane wrote, "There were no injuries, and the joy of the movement was palpable everywhere we went."[19]

A member of the women's collective at the *RAT Subterranean News* wrote, "When I heard about Whitehall being bombed I thought Right On – outasite to think that part of the movement that I was a part of had gotten their shit together and let Amerika know that they had talked and organized about not digging the draft system and all that it meant and stood for, long enough, and they really did mean it. And that act of bombing made sense to every Amerikan hearing and reading about it. They knew why kids would bomb Whitehall and they knew that act was in the name of millions of people in this country and that it followed a lot of demonstrations that got nowhere… A young kid coming around to draft age digs on the fact that someone was Robin-Hooding for him when that draft center got fucked over."[20]

"People on the streets outside the Induction Center had few doubts as to the political nature of the incident," the *RAT* reported. "One draft-aged man theorized that "a guy that didn't want to go" had done it, and smiled approvingly. Many older people stood around shaking their heads and saying that America was really in for it. One woman said, "I hope I'm not here to see it – America's really falling apart."[21]

A Deputy Fire Chief called it, "A terrific explosion. It devastated the fifth floor and blew out partitions."[22]

A witness working in the building explained, "It was like being back in Vietnam again. My first instinct was to run out of the building and that's what I did."[23]

The blast sent debris flying, shattering windows on adjacent buildings and littering the streets. It knocked out several walls and forty windows, broke water pipes, shut off electricity to the fifth floor, and ripped bricks and masonry from window ledges.[24]

The communiqué was minimal and had a different tone than the others. There was no attempt to explain the reasoning behind the bombing to supporters or the rest of the public. It was simply a declaration and a threat. But if this led to any doubt about its connection with the other bombings, it was soon put to rest when the bomb squad found another mainspring from a Westclox "Baby Ben" in the debris.[25]

> Tonight we bombed the Whitehall Induction Center.
> This action was in support of the N.L.F. [National Front for the Liberation of South Vietnam], legalized marijuana, love, Cuba, legalized abortion, and all the American revolutionaries and GIs who are winning the war against the Pentagon.
> Nixon, surrender now![26]

The action prevented hundreds of young men from being inducted into the war[27] and the building was eventually knocked down as a result of damages caused by the bombing. The Whitehall Induction Center was immediately closed, draftee physicals were postponed and induction operations were transferred to Brooklyn.[28]

It was especially surprising that anyone could get dynamite past the tight security in that building. At the entrance, two guards were checking bags, briefcases and parcels twenty-four hours a day, and other security were posted throughout the hallways. On top of that, pretty much everyone in the building was military.[29]

Later, Jane alluded that it was Dave Hughey who planned and carried out the Whitehall bombing while Sam was out of town.[30] The collective started falling apart shortly after the Federal

Building action, she claimed, because members, although they still agreed that further action was necessary, felt they had personally done enough. They had been arguing over whether or not it was a good idea to coordinate their next bombing with the upcoming National Mobilization Against the War protest, expected to be the biggest Anti-Vietnam War protest to date. The disagreement was serving as an exit strategy for some.

When Jane explained that a man from "the other group" wanted to use some dynamite to blow up the Whitehall Induction Center, the collective was as glad to see the dynamite go as they were in the United Fruit and Marine Midland bombings.[31]

By "the other group," Jane meant herself, Sam, Pat Swinton and Dave Hughey. Jane would take "the other group" over the collective any day of the week. It appears that during their time together at McCurdy's Place, Sam taught Dave what he knew about wiring up and planting bombs. But Sam had no intention of being tied down to any group. It seems he intended to be a sort of revolutionary version of Johnny Appleseed, teaching and helping people to become urban guerrillas and then moving on to do the same for someone else.

Going by Jane's accounts, Sam learned everything he could from the F.L.Q. fugitives, pulled together the collective to rob and maintain the dynamite, got another group together to bomb United Fruit, and hit Marine Midland on his own, in part, to inspire the collective to action. Finally the collective moved on the Federal Building. "The other group" bombed Whitehall and was already moving on to their next action with minimal participation from Sam.

Meanwhile, Sam was working on another bombing with a member of the collective who had been one of the Explo robbers,[32] and yet another bombing with a new recruit. Not only was Sam working with the members of the collective, the members of the "other group," a new recruit, and taking action on his own, but Jane wrote that Sam was out of town so much because he was at underground guerilla camps. These training camps, Jane said, were led by famed black militant of the Student Nonviolent Coordinating Committee and the Black Panther Party, H. Rap Brown.[33] There, she said, Sam met a Puerto Rican man and on September 24, 1969, they planted bombs in the Chicago Civic Center, the R.O.T.C. building at the University of Wisconsin and the National Guard office in Milwaukee's Federal Building.[34] Sam wasted no time. He was at war.

At about two a.m. on November 11th, 1969, bombs simultaneously exploded in three of Manhattan's largest skyscrapers.

> During this week of anti-war protest, we set off explosives in the offices of Chase Manhattan, Standard Oil, and General Motors. Guards at all three buildings and the news offices throughout the city were telephoned 30 to 40 minutes in advance to ensure that the buildings would be clear of people.
>
> The Vietnam War is only the most obvious evidence of the way this country's power destroys people. The giant corporations of America have now spread themselves all over the world, forcing entire foreign economies into total dependence on American money and goods.
>
> Here at home these same corporations have made us into insane consumers, devouring increasing quantities of useless credit cards and household appliances. We work at mindless jobs. Vast machines pollute our air, water and food.
>
> Spiro Agnew may be a household word, but it is the rarely seen men, like David Rockefeller of Chase Manhattan, James Roche of General Motors and Michael Haiden of Standard Oil, who run the system behind the scenes.
>
> The empire is breaking down as people all over the world are rising up to challenge its power. From the inside, black people have been fighting a revolution for years.
>
> And finally, from the heart of the empire, white Americans too are striking blows for liberation.[35]

The attack made national news.

Walter Cronkite introduced the story on *CBS*, "Bomb scares, including one at the United Nations building, swept through New York City today after early morning blasts in three skyscrapers. Police said the explosions were similar to those in private and government buildings here over the past three months."

The story was passed to a *CBS* correspondent, "The bombs exploded on the nineteenth floor of the new General Motors building on fashionable Fifth Avenue, on the sixteenth floor of the Chase Manhattan Bank's International headquarters in the financial district, on the twentieth floor of the RCA building in Rockefeller Center. Carefully coordinated, the explosives detonated shortly after one a.m. Most heavily damaged were the Standard Oil Company offices in the RCA building; walls blown apart, ceilings collapsed, elevator shafts heavily damaged. In each case the bombs were placed near elevators..."[36]

ABC called the bombings, "A protest against the Vietnam War and the power of giant American corporations throughout the world."

Their story featured a clip from an interview with the Vice President of Chase Manhattan bank, "The first word came by a phone call that was received at about 12:35, in that a male, harsh voice, indicated that three buildings in New York were going to be bombed and Chase was one of them."

ABC's correspondent wrapped the story up with a cliffhanger, "The F.B.I. is on the case and the city has assigned fifty detectives to it, and there are many rumors, but if anyone does have a valid lead to the bombers, he's certainly not making it public, at least at this moment."[37]

The movement didn't need any explanation as to why Standard Oil, Chase Manhattan and General Motors were bombed. Their roles were well known by anyone educated on U.S. imperialism or the Vietnam War.

Standard Oil of New Jersey was an offshoot of the original Standard Oil Trust founded by John D. Rockefeller, Sr. Anti-monopoly trust-busting legislation forced the Standard Oil

Trust to break into several companies, including Standard Oil of New Jersey, Standard Oil of Indiana, Standard Oil of California and Mobil Oil, which all still remained under the control of the Rockefellers. In 1969, Standard Oil of New Jersey operated in Venezuela under the subsidiary Creole Petroleum, and had virtually enslaved the Venezuelan economy, then the world's largest exporter and third largest producer of oil. Similar situations existed in Ecuador and Colombia, under their subsidiary, the International Petroleum Company. In most of the rest of the world, Standard Oil of New Jersey was better known by their Esso brand. The company was the world's largest overseas investor, operating in over 100 countries with 65,000 service stations and 126 oil tankers. In 1968, they were America's second largest industrial corporation, with sales of $13.3 billion.

Chase Manhattan was America's third largest commercial bank in 1969, with $20 billion in assets, 150 New York City area branches and 54 foreign branch banks. Chase was well known for giving financial aid to the atrocious apartheid regime in the Republic of South Africa and for their tremendous influence in the World Bank, where two of their chairmen had earned presidency. The board of directors of Chase Manhattan was an array of America's most powerful, including two presidents of Standard Oil, a former Secretary of the Treasury, and chairmen of Penn Central, Metropolitan Life, AT&T, General Foods and U.S. Steel.

The largest industrial corporation in America was General Motors, with 1968 sales reaching $14 million. Its chairman, James M. Rouche, had the highest salary of any corporate executive - $794,934. Mobil Oil, Standard Oil of New Jersey and Gulf all had directors in General Motors. Besides producing five brand names of automobiles in the U.S. and five outside the country, the company was the tenth largest defense contractor nationally, producing engines for close-support fighter-bombers and Main Battle Tanks.[38]

The sixty-story Chase Manhattan Plaza was only eight years old when a warning call led to the evacuation of the bank's 1,300 night clerks.

> There will be three bombs going off
> in New York tonight. One will be in Chase
> Manhattan Plaza. For the safety of your people,
> clear floors 13-24.[39]

The bomb blasted out of a locker opposite an elevator on the 16th floor, the bank's international department. The blast wrecked three elevators and blew debris through the elevator shaft onto the 15th floor and the 17th floor,[40] where the bank's executive office suites were located, including the suite of Chase Manhattan's board chairman, David Rockefeller.[41]

The Rockefellers also owned a large number of shares in the Standard Oil Company, whose government relations department offices on the 20th floor of the RCA building at Rockefeller Center were bombed that night as well.

A maintenance man working in the RCA building at the time of that explosion described it as, "One hell of a big noise and it scared me to death."[42]

The glass and marble structure was only one year old at the time of the explosion and, standing at 70-stories tall, it was the fifth highest building in New York City and the sixth highest in the country.

"There is extensive damage to an area 30 feet by 100 feet," a Deputy Fire Chief explained, "Almost an entire suite of offices was damaged. There is extensive damage to a whole bank of six elevators. Walls are blown in. Doors and partitions too, and all the window glass was blown out."[43]

The blast sent shards of glass raining down on the street and an empty elevator plummeting to the ground floor.[44]

The scene on the 19th floor of the 50-story General Motors building was more of the same, knocking two elevators out of commission and destroying walls. The two soda machines that the bomb was planted between were badly twisted out of shape.[45] It blew out a cinder-block wall, exterior doors and walls of the elevator shafts, mail chutes, air ducts, and the doors of stockrooms and offices.[46]

A Deputy Police Chief on the scene testified, "It was a forceful explosion. It was no child's toy."[47]

VIETNAM IN MANHATTAN

"New York can take almost anything in stride, including a bombing a month," said the New York Police Department's Chief of Detectives, "but with the simultaneous explosions at GM, RCA, and the Chase Bank, the town suddenly got a case of the jitters."[48]

Increased security measures were already in effect because of the previous attacks and officials at all three buildings expressed amazement that anyone could pull these bombings off.[49] An investigator told the press, "Whoever is behind this is extremely methodical and very well informed."[50]

A bomb squad Lieutenant said, "Something like this unleashes every nut in the city,"[51] and over 200 bomb threats were phoned in before the day was through.[52]

The U.S. Federal Building, Army Induction Center, Chase Manhattan, Standard Oil, and General Motors attacks all went off as planned. The bombs wrecked their targets, there were no injuries to speak of and the bombers remained at large. In less than two months, five Manhattan buildings involved in the Vietnam war were torn apart by dynamite. The next step that everyone in the struggle was whispering about had arrived. Revolution was erupting in the United States. Vietnam had been brought to Manhattan.

4

NOVEMBER 12, 1969

Sam peeked through the shades of his apartment with the lights off, trying to keep an eye on the white Mercury sedan parked outside. It was the same car that he'd seen sitting out there for the past two nights with men inside, watching. They didn't look like the kind of guys you'd expect to see hanging out in the East Village. They took turns, one staying in the car while the other got out to stretch his legs or get some coffee. Sam was convinced they were bomb squad.[1]

In the stairwell of his apartment weeks before, he tried to shake some F.B.I. men by giving them a fake name. They were looking for Sam Melville, who was he? "David McCurdy."[2]

He should have realized that "David McCurdy" had just received a copy of his birth certificate though the U.S. Postal Service to Pat Swinton's address, that "David McCurdy" had rented the apartment where the dynamite was hidden. Now it was too late. If the F.B.I. figured out that "David McCurdy" was the name on Sam's false identification, they would also suspect Pat and find the address of McCurdy's Place. At any moment they could burst into his and Jane's apartment, Pat's apartment, or maybe worst of all, McCurdy's Place, where they would find not just the stolen Explo dynamite and blasting caps, but wires, wire cutters, electrical tape, nine-volt batteries, Westclox "Big Ben" alarm clocks, newspaper articles covering the bombings, a book on military explosives, even a live M-26 fragmentation hand grenade and small arsenal of guns Sam had collected and stored there over the months, including a 9 mm automatic pistol, a .30-caliber carbine rifle, two 9 mm submachine guns and hundreds of rounds of ammunition.[3]

Jane came in the door and Sam quickly put his finger to his lips, "Shhhh! They're back!"

It was the evening of November 12, 1969, and Sam had just gotten home himself. He had been out that day planting another bomb with a member of the defunct collective, and sending the media a communiqué.

COURTHOUSE TO BE BOMBED AT 9 P.M.
WARNING TO EVACUATE WILL BE GIVEN
The establishment is in for some big

surprises if it thinks that kangaroo courts and death sentences can arrest a revolution. The anger of youth and all oppressed people is mounting against this mockery of justice. There's one thing the cowards who rule this world might as well know: the will to freedom of the people is stronger than the fear of any repression. Liberty or death![4]

The bomb exploded on the 4th floor of the Criminal Court building on Centre Street, across the street from the Federal Building they'd bombed less than two months earlier. The target was the site of a conspiracy trial against The Panther 21.

The trial was one of the biggest cases against the Black Panther Party and was being watched closely by the whole country. 21 New York City Panthers were rounded up on April 2, 1969, and charged with a conspiracy to blow up department stores and even the Bronx Botanical Gardens. It was the beginning of a nationwide crackdown on the Black Panther Party, including police raids on Panther offices and homes in Philadelphia, Chicago, Newark, Omaha, Denver, New Haven, San Diego, Los Angeles, and elsewhere. The police and the media portrayed the Panthers as a violent and irrational organization, but the movement saw the trial as a clear frame-up. Why would the Panthers want to blow up department stores and a botanical garden? It didn't make any sense. The defendants were held for two years before they were finally acquitted of all charges.[5]

The explosion at the courthouse destroyed a seventy-foot terra cotta wall, ripped steel doors from their hinges and covered Centre Street in shards of broken glass and debris. To add to the damage, the bomb was placed behind a plumbing access panel. Water from the broken pipes flooded the halls and flowed down into the main lobby. The scene looked so much like the Marine Midland, the Federal Building, the Whitehall Army Induction Center, the Chase Manhattan Bank Tower, the Standard Oil and the General Motors explosions that investigators knew what to expect before they arrived, and were getting frustrated. Once again, nobody was caught, and nobody was injured.[6] Prisoners held in another part of the building heard and felt the explosion, and were ordered back to their cells.[7]

Sam and Jane planned to close out their bank accounts and skip town the next day. They sensed danger closing in on them. H. Rap Brown was about to hold another secret training camp on a farm in the middle of nowhere. After it was over they planned to ask the owners of the farm if they could hide out there for the winter. But Sam had another bombing planned before he would leave. Jane tried to convince him it was too risky, that he should skip it.

"No. I promised George I'd meet him."[8]

Sam first met George Demmerle during a brief stop at the Woodstock festival. Demmerle was dressed in a purple cape and a pink, feathered helmet, manning the Crazies' booth in the Movement City section of the festival, selling buttons. Movement City was an area on the festival grounds dedicated to social and political causes far off from the main activities. The Crazies were a group that took after Abbie Hoffman's Yippies, with street theater and humorous political campaigns like running a turkey in the race for Mayor of New York City.

Demmerle held a leadership role in the Crazies and had been involved in the Free School of New York, Progressive Labor in Brooklyn, the Yippies, Veterans and Reservists to End the War in Vietnam, the New York Young Patriots, the United Front Conference in Oakland, and even the violent Days of Rage actions in Chicago, organized by a militant offshoot of Students for a Democratic Society called the Weathermen.[9]

Demmerle was older than almost everybody else there, even a few years older than Sam. He manned the Crazies' booth for long hours without sitting down and impressed Sam with his dedication. Demmerle said he came from a working class family and, like Sam, abandoned his straight life to join the movement as an adult. To top it off, Demmerle had all kinds of wild sabotage ideas, including blowing up the Brooklyn Bridge and dropping a powerful chemical into telephone manholes in Manhattan to eat away at the electronic communication network that the financial district relied on.[10] Sam took him under his wing.

The two had arranged to do their first action that evening.

NOVEMBER 12, 1969

Sam devised a clever scheme to bomb a National Guard armory without ever entering the building. During the day a number of Army trucks were parked outside along the street, and every night they were brought inside the armory. All they had to do was set the bombs to explode late that night, plant them in the trucks, and let the National Guard do the rest of the work for them.[11] It was a simple initiation that would test Demmerle's seriousness and commitment to the struggle.

Sam kissed Jane and left their apartment wearing a military jacket with colonel's stripes, and a matching duffle bag over his shoulder.[12]

At McCurdy's Place, Demmerle watched as Sam wired four bombs and packed them into his duffle bag. They avoided the front door by exiting onto the roof, crossing over six apartment buildings and coming out through a door on the other side of the block. They left heading in different directions.

Sam stopped at a deli on 4th Avenue to have a sandwich and something to drink, and then swung by a hangout popular with students from Cooper Union and New York University. At about 9:30 p.m. he got on the subway and took the #4 local train heading north.

The bomb had just exploded at the Criminal Courts building less than an hour before. The bomb squad and whoever else was on the case would be busy downtown, scratching their heads and sifting through the debris. Sam whistled, making his way uptown.

He got off the subway at 23rd Street and Park Avenue, and headed east on 23rd. He turned up Lexington Avenue towards 25th Street, where he had Demmerle positioned on a corner to notice if he was being followed. He passed right by Demmerle without acknowledging him and turned down 26th street to the 68th Regiment Armory.

Sam circled around on Lexington again for Demmerle who was still on 25th, keeping an eye out. They spoke briefly and then walked on opposite sides of the street towards the armory where three army trucks were parked along the curb.[13]

Then Sam noticed something was wrong. The trucks were on the wrong side of the street, near a row of private houses. They were always parked on the side near the armory when he cased the scene.

He couldn't risk the dynamite exploding so close to innocent people. What if the routine was changed and they didn't bring the trucks inside that night? What if they were onto him? He turned around and started walking away.

Suddenly men burst out from around every corner with guns drawn. There were dozens of them. Sam was surrounded.

The F.B.I. had wanted to catch Sam in the act to ensure a solid conviction, but they just couldn't keep tabs on him. They frequently lost track of him for days on end, and even with N.Y.P.D. detectives added to the surveillance team that day, he was able to slip away long enough to plant a bomb that wrecked the Criminal Courthouse. If he got away now maybe they would never see him again. They couldn't risk it. When Sam turned back without planting a bomb, they jumped.

The agents were frantic. One yelled, "Drop it!" and another replied, "No! No! Don't drop it for Christ's sake!" fearing the bomb would go off. Then he put his ear to Sam's ticking duffle bag and started screaming for the bomb squad.

"Relax," Sam said, "They're not set to go off until [four] o'clock."[14]

5 A RELIABLE SOURCE

A team of 25 F.B.I. agents and 25 N.Y.P.D. detectives were assigned to make the arrests at the armory.[1] They held Sam against the wall while searching him, finding a .38 caliber five-shot revolver, a penknife, and a tear gas pen. They removed four bombs from his duffle bag, each made of four to six sticks of dynamite wired to blasting caps, nine-volt batteries and Westclox "Big Ben" alarm clocks. Once the bombs were disarmed they inspected the serial numbers on the dynamite and blasting caps.

"This is the Explo dynamite stolen in July," a detective announced on the spot, "and those are the Explo blasting caps."[2]

They took Sam's keys and loose change and cuffed his hands behind his back before putting him and Demmerle in the back seat of an unmarked blue Chevrolet[3] and taking them to be strip-searched and interrogated.

Sam was in an interview room with a metal table and three chairs. The agents seemed frightened of him, only addressing him to order that he assume a position. He was cooperative, but hadn't spoken at all.

"What's your name?" asked the youngest agent in a friendly voice.

"Sam Melville."

"Is it Samuel?"

"Yes."

He gave 67 East 2nd Street as his home address, McCurdy's Place, trying not to lead the agents to any of the others. He intended to take the fall alone, like Pierre Vallieres did for the F.L.Q. fugitives Sam harbored just six months earlier.

A second agent was writing it all down and a third was going through Sam's telephone book before leaving the room with it. The first two listed his confiscated possessions on an envelope and had him sign it.

The second agent was examining the tear gas pen. Sam warned him not to set it off and talked him through the process of carefully unscrewing the capsule while not releasing the spring to safely disarm it.

"Sam, my name is Tom," said the first agent, who Sam guessed was about thirty years old, "Can I get you some coffee?"

A RELIABLE SOURCE

"Okay," Sam replied and asked for some water too. Agent Tom left the room to fetch the beverages.

The second agent told Sam he could call him "Bob" and became friendly as well, offering Sam a cigarette as he took one himself. Sam didn't smoke.

"Well, Sam, you gave us quite a time."

Sam nodded and smiled, attempting to predict their next move. It seemed agent Bob wasn't capable of torture, none of them were, he thought.

"You were good. You had this office jumping for months."

Agent Bob was making an obvious attempt to please Sam and started running through the laundry list of bombings, but suddenly changed his tone at the Criminal Courthouse that blew earlier that night.

"You know that guy might die?" he baited Sam.

"What guy?"

"The courthouse. You know, 100 Centre St."

"Did it go? What do you mean about the guy dying?" Sam took the bait.

"Yeah, he may lose his arm."

Sam plummeted into concern and sorrow. He told them he never tried to hurt anyone but the agents argued that he must have known someone would get injured when he planted the bombs in the armory trucks.

Sam explained what happened in a letter to his lawyers, "I said I never put the bomb in the truck and wasn't going to. The trucks were on the wrong side of the street opposite the armory. There were private homes on that side. On four previous nights when I cased the job, the trucks were always on the curb immediately adjacent to the armory. I think the trucks were placed so it would appear that I cared little about people's safety. When I saw the trucks that night I decided I was not going to do it. When I was arrested I was in fact walking away from the trucks with the bombs still on my person."

"What about the people at the bank building?" the agents prodded, referring to injuries from the Marine Midland bombing.

"I never intended to hurt anyone," Sam repeated himself,

then he asked to see his lawyer. The agents said that it was too late an hour and they wouldn't be able to reach his lawyer until the morning.

"This is strictly off the record, Sam," agent Tom said, still friendly and even comforting towards Sam in his apparent distress, "Did you intend to use the gun?"

Sam laughed a little and told them no. He wasn't even sure if it worked. It was pretty old and he never fired it. He figured he was carrying it to impress himself. He was sinking. They knew they had him.[4]

Right after Sam and Demmerle were arrested, thirty agents came banging on the door of Jane and Sam's apartment at 235 East 4th Street. Jane was there with Dave, listening to the breaking radio reports of the Criminal Courthouse blast and waiting for Sam to get back.

"Open up! We've got your friend!"

The plaster around the hinges was cracking from the agents forcing the door when Jane finally unlocked the deadbolt. The agents came storming into the apartment, slammed Jane against the wall and announced, "It's [Hughey], it's [Hughey],"[5] after they got Dave in handcuffs.

They immediately tore the place up in a search while other agents took Jane and Dave to separate unmarked cars and tried to fight back a couple of concerned neighbors and a growing crowd of spectators gathering in front of the apartment building.

In Jane and Sam's apartment they found a map of the Bronx with the Explo site circled, stacks of revolutionary pamphlets, stolen passports, a box of .38 caliber bullets and a rifle. It wasn't much compared to what they would find at McCurdy's Place.

Pat's apartment was in the same building. Her door hung wide open as Jane and Dave were dragged out to the street.

Jane and Dave were taken to the F.B.I. offices at 201 East 69th Street where Sam and Demmerle were already being questioned. Jane was put in a small room.

"Where did you go to school, Jane?"

"Do you have any brothers or sisters?"

A RELIABLE SOURCE

"How long have you lived on 4th Street?"

Jane didn't budge. She answered every question with, "I want to talk to my lawyer," and wouldn't even give her name.

On her way to be photographed and fingerprinted she crossed Sam in the hall. He looked defeated. She mouthed to him to call their lawyer but he couldn't make out what she was trying to say.[6]

Until Sam saw Jane in custody at the F.B.I. building he hoped just he and Demmerle were busted. The sight further broke his resolve.

As we left the room I saw Jane and thought all was lost. I was very discouraged and began to talk very freely. They asked if I wrote the press releases. I said yes. I said I did everything alone. Telephone calls, writing and placing of the bombs... Bob then showed me a form which informed me of my rights. I read it but I don't remember what it said. I think it was a triplicate. I signed all of them... Bob said he was going to read me a statement he had written. If I agreed with it, would I sign it? I said yes. He then read a two or three page statement that listed all the jobs plus a couple I had never heard about... I said I wouldn't sign it. He then crossed out the two I said I hadn't done and again asked me to sign it. I looked it over and realized it was a confession. I said I wouldn't sign it.[7]

Just that day an article ran in the *New York Post* about how police were leaning towards a "one-man theory," claiming that the bombings at United Fruit, Marine Midland, the Federal Building, the Whitehall Induction Center, General Motors, Chase Manhattan and Standard Oil were likely to be the work of a single man.

"Evidence thus far points to the bomber as a middle-aged white man who is well-informed on current events and financial and business matters and who identifies with Leftist causes," the article read. "The one-man theory appears further supported by the failure of undercover agents and informants in militant or politically oriented groups of all shades of opinion to obtain information linking these organizations to the bombings... Similar timing devices were found at each of the explosion sites, indicating a link between [the General Motors, Chase Manhattan, and Standard Oil] blasts and the four earlier ones."[8]

The next morning, the *New York Post* announced the arrests and a conspiracy of five – Sam, Demmerle, Jane, Dave, and Pat. They raided Pat's apartment too, but she was out on a date with the Puerto Rican man Sam had met at H. Rap Brown's guerrilla training camp and brought home to New York after their Mid-West bombing spree. She somehow caught news of the shake down while out and slipped away.[9]

ABC broadcast the arrests across the nation, "Men carrying a duffle bag came to this armory last night. It was dark and quiet when they threw the bag into the last Army truck and started to walk away[10]. But that was as far as they got without sudden police escort and later, charges of conspiracy in eight bombings in New York City. Two other persons were later arrested and a third is being hunted. F.B.I. and city detectives said they trailed the men on a subway from a dingy apartment on the city's Lower East Side. After their arrests, police returned to the apartment and arrested two other suspects, one of them a young lady. At their federal arraignment today bail for each one was set at a half million dollars, none could raise it. The two arrested at the scene were thirty-four-year-old Samuel Melville, who said he had a prior record and was carrying a revolver at the time of his arrest, and thirty-nine-year-old George Demmerle, who said he was an unemployed die-maker. In the apartment the F.B.I. had arrested twenty-two-year-old Jane Alpert, a recent Swarthmore College graduate who wrote for one of the city's underground newspapers, and John Hughey III, a twenty-two-year-old from Sumpter, South Carolina, who also wrote for the underground press in New York. A second woman, Pat Swinton, is also charged and the F.B.I. is looking for her."[11]

The only information the F.B.I. could give on Pat was that she was twenty-two years old, lived at 235 East 4th Street and worked for the North American Congress on Latin America. Then they took it back, saying they weren't positive if she really lived at the address and weren't even sure if the North American Congress on Latin America existed, telling the press, "We really don't know."[12]

They told reporters that Jane was a twenty-two year old writer and researcher who often spent 10-12 hours a day working for an underground newspaper. They described her as "a tall, slim young woman with hazel eyes and brown hair cut in the pixie style," adding that she had written articles opposing the draft, the war in Vietnam, the Pledge of Allegiance in schools, abortion laws and "feminist inequalities," and had been telling friends she was planning on heading down to Washington D.C. for a large protest scheduled against the Vietnam War the weekend of the arrests.

The *New York Times* quoted an associate of Jane's saying, "She liked being in the vanguard of various activities, and she was to the left of most members of the women's liberation movement, but she is very gentle, pretty, and she doesn't look like a hard militant type. She speaks very sincerely – a good educated voice," but her co-workers at *RAT Subterranean News* spoke only of a conspiracy of the F.B.I. to "stifle dissent and punish representatives of the anti-establishment movement."[13]

Reporters described Dave as the estranged twenty-two year old son of a southern Baptist Reverend, born in Sumpter, South Carolina, who spent twelve years in Switzerland with his family, graduated from Thomas Jefferson High School in Richmond with honors, and enrolled in Duke University on a scholarship. The press mistakenly spoke of Dave as Jane's "old man," even claiming that they lived together.

"We have not been in touch with him since he dropped out of Duke University in 1966," Dave's father told the New York Times, adding that their numerous efforts to contact him brought no response.

The papers printed that he was slender, intelligent, introverted, quiet, gentle and likable, and since college he had worked for Greyhound Bus Lines and most recently in the art department of the radical weekly, *The Guardian*.[14]

Sam was "the alleged ring leader, who the F.B.I. said

fashioned the bombs out of stolen dynamite." [15] At thirty-four years old he was described as standing six foot one, weighing 180 pounds and wearing a tattered Air Force jacket.

An owner of the Syska & Hennessy, Inc., engineering firm that employed Sam for nearly three years, told reporters that Sam's work record was average and that he had no idea why Sam up and left his mid-level position, something between a draftsman and an engineer, in late 1966. His records showed that Sam claimed to have graduated from Amherst Central High School in Buffalo, attended Brooklyn Polytechnic Institute in 1961-1962 and worked for three other engineering firms in New York City between 1955 and 1963.

"They came here because of the cheap rent," The landlord at McCurdy's Place told the press of his tenants, "They came here to do their thing, some of them came to paint or write and others maybe came to make bombs," but he insisted that Sam was always a gentleman.

He said Sam was, "a quiet one... a health nut who liked sunlight," and that he lifted weights and left town frequently. He noticed that the man who would watch Sam's apartment when he was out of town was arrested as part of the conspiracy. It was Dave. [16]

The U.S. Attorney argued that the defendants "have shown wanton disregard for the safety of the community," [17] adding that they committed "a most serious crime." At the arraignment he convinced the judge to issue a bench warrant for the arrest of Pat and hold the other four on an astonishing half a million dollars bail each, claiming, "The nature of the charge makes it appear not only that very substantial damage was done to property but that the lives of hundreds of people were endangered." [18]

The suddenness of the arrests and indictments raised suspicions that there might be an informant in the mix. Just two days earlier, the *New York Times* ran their faulty "one-man theory" article and now everything had changed. Reporters pressed to get the scoop on what happened in-between.

"I cannot answer that now," was all the Assistant Director of the F.B.I. would say about the role of undercover work in the investigation on the day of the arrest, but the next day he elaborated, "Agents had information that caused them to place these people under surveillance." In the paperwork he filed with the U.S. Commissioner he specified that this information came "from a reliable source."

Reliable indeed. On the morning before the arrests, two F.B.I. agents wearing pullover sweaters and dungarees, calling themselves "Mikey" and "Terry," staked out the East 4th Street apartment building from an air-conditioner repair shop across the street with the consent of its owner. They shaved two sets of eyeholes into the painted windows of the shop for their binoculars and set up their radio transmitter/receivers. They put photographs of the suspects, taken at anti-war demonstrations, under the eyeholes, to help make positive identifications.

Twenty-eight other agents were spread out over the surrounding ten-block area. When Jane left the apartment her every move was followed and transmitted by an agent on a motorcycle, but they failed to keep tabs on Pat. When they got word that Sam and Demmerle were arrested they sprung the trap on Jane and Dave. [19]

The *Times* described Demmerle as a thirty-nine year old unemployed diemaker of medium height, brown eyes and brown hair. His family all said they had little contact with him in recent years and all seemed to have different opinions of him, ranging from a loner to outgoing and from left-wing to right-wing.

"I was probably closer than anyone to him, and we weren't very close," his brother Walter said. "I thought he was to the right from the way he talked. How, if he got to the left, I don't know."

When reporters told Demmerle's brother Richard about his arrest with seven others who were attempting to disrupt former U.S. Vice President Hubert H. Humphrey's speech at a Commodore Hotel luncheon that April 19th, Richard was in shock. "You're talking to me of an altogether different person – a side of him I never knew of."[20]

In the movement, Demmerle was best known as "Prince Crazy," a familiar sight marching for the Crazies on Eighth Street and Sixth Avenue in his lavender jeweled suit and pink helmet with feather dusters attached atop like a Roman guard. He was also popular for his role as a mad anarchist in the Yippie street theater skit, Pigasus For President, where he was tossed into the Hudson River for trying to throw a classic little black bomb at the pig the Yippies were sarcastically endorsing for the U.S. Presidency. Others knew of him from organizing benefits for the Panther 21.

At a bail hearing shortly after the arrests, George Demmerle was released on his own recognizance and identified as an informant.

Suddenly, a lot of things made sense beyond the unexpected break in the case. Factionalism had seemed to surround Demmerle's involvement in groups like the Young Patriots and the Revolutionary Contingent and, although he had no known source of income, he frequently flew to Chicago around the time of the Weathermen's Days of Rage. A number of specific circumstances, like raids on Weathermen he had close contact with, fueled the paranoia and some people even speculated that all the Crazies were cops who flashed their Crazy buttons at police during protests as a secret sign of allegiance.

More grounded were peoples' suspicions of Demmerle's conflicting viewpoints on violence. At times he would speak openly, in hushed tones, about explosives in New Jersey, Chicago, upstate New York and Queens, and at other times he would go on one-man peace crusades, trying to save groups like the Weathermen "from their own violence." A number of people who knew Demmerle were less than shocked, and even warned Sam not to trust him. Nobody seemed to know much of anything about his personal background.[21]

Up until Demmerle was exposed as an informant, the movement seemed to think the F.B.I. could be spotted a mile away. On July 25, 1970, Yippie leader Jerry Rubin wrote about the effect this news had on him.

We knew pigs could memorize a lot of ideological crap and mechanically rap revolution.

But no pig would grow his hair long.

A RELIABLE SOURCE

No pig would smoke dope and maintain his cover.

No pig could run with the outrageous antics of the street theater Yippies and Crazies. Then came George Demmerle...

George was the craziest cat around. If you wanted anything flippy done, call George...

One day George said he had something very important to talk to me about...

He said the revolution had to go beyond street theater into real disruption and he had this groovy plan to blow up the Brooklyn Bridge...

When the New York bombers were finally caught, after frightening the city for weeks with brilliant attacks on key capitalist symbols, setting off thousands of bomb scares and forcing paranoid building after paranoid building to stop its work, empty its inhabitants into the streets and search the premises, a group of bombers was arrested. George was one of them.

I thought to myself, "Yeh, [sic] George was crazy enough to do something as brave as that. You got to be a little crazy to be so brave"...

Then a day later I read that George was released without bail on the prosecution's motion and he was going to testify for the government. My heart stopped. I felt so shitty.

George's emergence as an F.B.I. informer for eight years dealt a temporary blow to the freaky movement in New York. The Crazies broke up. A lot of the young kids whom George had recruited into the movement disappeared. Only the most committed could withstand the shock. Remember Prince Crazy and all his funny uniforms? He always came to demonstrations dressed in purple hats and capes. Well, he was a John Birch Society member [a national, right wing, pro-American,

anti-communist organization], and maybe even
possibly a Minuteman, who infiltrated the
movement and stayed up late every night filing
reports for the F.B.I.[22]

According to court testimony, Demmerle approached an F.B.I.
special agent during the summer of 1966 to volunteer his services.
He had recently left the Minutemen, a militant right-wing group
founded in the early 1960s to counteract a perceived communist
takeover of the U.S.[23] He had decided that the Minutemen were
"no more an answer to America's problems than the Communist
Party."

They set up a deal where Demmerle wrote weekly reports
for the F.B.I. on each of the individuals and organizations he got
in with. They started off giving him $50 for each report, but by
the time of the arrest it had gone up to $250 each, plus expenses.
Demmerle's history of mental instability, displayed by a string of
institutionalizations detailed in his F.B.I. dossier, was somehow
considered irrelevant to the accuracy and value of the information
he provided and was never allowed to be produced in court.[24]

In a press conference held in the lobby of the Manhattan
Center, Demmerle bragged about how easy it was for him as a spy
over the years and claimed to be motivated by patriotism, "What
kind of person am I? It's very simple. I care about this country, I
care about the people."

> Q: I have one last question for you. You
> spent six years more or less living as a hippie,
> as a person in the East Village. Now you're back
> living as a straight. How much of your East
> Village hippie-yippie lifestyle are you going to
> continue?
> A: A lot of it I dig.
> Q: Like what?
> A: Mm... No comment.[25]

After testifying, Demmerle collected a $25,000 reward from
Marine Midland Bank for information leading to the arrest of their

bomber and again disappeared without a trace.[26]

6
COURTROOM
HISTRIONICS

MAD BOMBER MELVILLE

After about a week of pre-trial court proceedings, defense lawyers successfully convinced Judge Milton Pollack to lower bail from half a million dollars each to $20,000 each for Jane and Dave, and $50,000 for Sam. Jane and Dave were bailed out and supporters went to work raising money for legal fees and Sam's release.

So all week [the staff of *RAT Subterranean News*] spent our time protesting the innocence of Jane Alpert, Dave Hughey, and Sam Melville. "A classic case of the government entrapping the three by using an agent." Expediency insists that you carefully lay out the facts of the case to the mass media and to people who might give bail money, but your insides scream at their civilized know-nothingism. You don't want to talk about innocence in the New York bombings, though you believe it to be true, you want to rip off their ties, hit them in the stomach to get a little emotion flowing...

Eight bombings destroyed corporate property in New York. In the Vietnamese Demilitarized Zone the U.S. Air Force has dropped 500 pounds of bombs for every person...

Reporters question: "Was she the violent type, you know, was there anything in her past which suggests that she might be involved in extremist behavior?" Answer: "She was outgoing and thoughtfully friendly, blah, blah, blah..."

Quiet Paul Meadlo, of Terre Haute, Indiana, tells the nation he has shot old men, women and children with his M-16 while on duty in Vietnam. Townspeople and neighbors insist Paul has always been a nice boy. Not a troublemaker. It's a shame what happened in Vietnam. One of those things...

When we called people for money for

legal defense some moaned about the polarization of the country; they didn't like it. Getting involved with people charged with bombings was somehow too sticky. You had the feeling that innocence or guilt didn't so much matter. If the problem would just go away, the people quietly go to jail, everything would be more comfortable for them. They didn't want anything to disturb the parade for peace in Washington... It was somehow safer to gather in the eclipse and sing along... "All we are saying, is give peace a chance."[1]

From the beginning of the proceedings, the defense argued a motion to dismiss Sam's confession, which wasn't recorded and mostly occurred after F.B.I. agents Bob and Tom denied Sam's request to speak with his lawyer, telling him it was too late an hour. On Wednesday, December 31, 1969, Sam testified that he didn't know that what he was saying to the agents could be used against him in court, and he held to it under cross-examination. This forced the government to produce several F.B.I. agents in court whose testimony all conflicted, but the judge still ruled to allow the confession.

At 3 p.m. on Friday, January 2, 1970, Sam's support committee went to the bondsman's office with the money raised to bail him out. In just two hours U.S. Attorney John Doyle responded by requesting Sam's bail be raised to $150,000, arguing that "the weight of evidence is now overwhelmingly against the defendant."

The only new evidence was an article printed in *RAT Subterranean News* encouraging readers to contribute to Sam's defense fund. An excerpt from the last paragraph drew the attention of the prosecution and the judge, "There is only one position the movement can take in relation to Sam Melville: either he is totally innocent of the charges filed against him and is the victim of a repressive government frame-up, or he is a dedicated and courageous revolutionary brother and must be set free at any cost. In either case, he must go free."

The judge feared that Sam would jump bail because he had little connection to the people contributing money to his bail fund and that the defense committee wanted nothing more than to see Sam bomb more buildings. Questioning the contributors to Sam's bail fund in court only reinforced his suspicions. After hearing the prosecution's argument that Sam's supporters were urging him to flee and do "whatever this so-called revolution demanded," the judge raised Sam's bail to $100,000.[2]

When supporters came back with the additional $50,000, the judge insisted that a wealthy individual put up the entire bail unassisted and take full responsibility for Sam while the trial was still pending. By the time such a person was produced Sam was being taken to the same Criminal Court building that he bombed the day of his arrest, to be indicted on the state charges. The state charges didn't allow for bail, so Sam wasn't released.[3]

The prosecutor wouldn't budge on a thirty-year minimum sentence for Sam until the day before the trial was scheduled to start. Rather than risk the public spectacle of taking the case to trial, the prosecutor offered fifteen years for Sam and five years each for Jane and Dave under the condition that all three entered guilty pleas. Sam got word to Jane and Dave urging them to plea so he could get a release date before he grew to be an old man.

"I don't have much hope of a so-called political trial," Sam wrote from prison, "I'm not sure I ever did. Folks are either beyond needing that kind of education or it will never move them anyway. That's not to imply I'm discouraged. I'm just getting realistic. With repression getting heavier folks have to move beyond the kangaroos [courts]. I find it laughable that we can still have papers printing info on [Molotov] cocktails and other things. Anyway, I hope the home fires keep burning."[4]

"I have little to say regarding our last court appearance and it's possible effect," Sam continued in a later letter, "I just don't think folks need further demonstrations of the court's bankruptcy... Ours is not a political case. We aren't testing the letter or intent of the law. The law is our enemy. With one's enemy it is sometimes expedient to make deals. But to be forced to acknowledge their procedure and rhetoric without denying their authority would be treachery."[5]

"Hanging over all our legal decisions was the fact that Sam faced more than three hundred years in total time," Jane wrote, "The more political we made the trial, the worse the consequences would have been for Sam... It would have made a splash in the papers perhaps; but Sam did not want to spend his life in prison for the sake of verbal histrionics. He hated the courtroom. When he was not completely ignoring the proceedings he sat with his fists clenched and his mouth tightened in barely suppressed fury."[6]

"The first few weeks she was out we had no trouble keeping track of Jane Alpert," recalled the Chief of N.Y.P.D. detectives, "Every day she religiously attended the proceedings of the so-called Panther 21 trial. Using her *RAT* press card, she got a front row seat among the rest of the reporters."[7]

The N.Y.P.D. detectives didn't catch on that Jane was also spending some of what would be her last free time with Weathermen who were taking inspiration from the bombings. The Weathermen were in the process of evolving into the Weather Underground and were preparing to use some dynamite of their own instead of staying above ground and facing criminal charges from their violent Days of Rage protests in Chicago. They wanted Jane to skip out on her sentencing date and join them.

On March 6, 1970, a series of explosions erupted in a Greenwich Village townhouse on 18 East 11th Street. The house was owned by the father of Weatherman Cathy Wilkerson, and was being used as a bomb factory for the organization. The dynamite was set off accidentally, killing Ted Gold, Diana Oughton and Terry Robbins, and injuring Cathy Wilkerson and Kathy Boudin. Wilkerson and Boudin managed to escape before the police arrived but the explosion forced the Weathermen underground prematurely, before plans could be finalized with Jane. [8]

On May 8, 1970, Sam, Jane and Dave all pled guilty to a federal conspiracy.

Sam only made one comment during sentencing his last day in court. When the judge emphasized the damage Sam caused by pointing out that one of his bombings destroyed $90,000 in property, Sam stood up and shouted, "That's about two Viet

Cong!" referring to an estimate that it was costing the U.S. government about $35,000 for each Viet Cong guerrilla it killed.[9]

Sam was sentenced to thirteen years for the federal charges and eighteen years for the state charges. The sentences were to run concurrently. With good time, Sam could be out in his mid-fifties.

A few days later, shortly before her sentencing, with Pat already on the run and the Weathermen nowhere to be found, Jane jumped bail and joined the swelling underground.[10]

Page 28 of the May 22nd issue of *RAT Subterranean News* featured a full-page drawing of a note to Jane that read, "DEAR JANE, YOU LEFT THE WATER RUNNING. love, the RAT collective. P.S. ALL POWER TO UNDERGROUND SISTERS."

An earlier article titled "All the Low Down on the Blow Down" illustrated the way much of the movement felt about the bombings.

> The bombs which have shaken New York City for five months ripped into the steel and concrete guts of Amerika. They exploded in the office buildings and corporate headquarters where the business of the Amerikan empire is carried out.
>
> Each day those buildings suck in human energy and spit it out again in a regular nine-to-five rhythm. Then they stand idle and aloof, empty of humanity, while the rest of Manhattan swells to the point of explosion. During the day, the decisions made and carried out in these anonymous executive suites and administrative offices affect the lives of millions of people. It is important to examine the particulars of their functioning.

The article explained that the Whitehall Induction Center, the Criminal Courthouse and the Federal Building were "understandable enough" as bombing targets. Whitehall, it said, "takes the men who are needed in Amerika's wars," the courthouse

COURTROOM HISTRIONICS

"flushes away the men and women who are dysfunctional," and the Federal Building "is the embodiment of the Amerikan government, spreading its bureaucratic pall over the nation."

It explained that the corporate targets were less clear to most Americans, who "are not meant to understand the workings of Chase Manhattan or General Motors, and ideally they are brought up not to care."

> Those private corporate entities house the men who make the critical decisions about the economic life of the empire. They live in fancy estates like the Rockefeller's Pocantico in Terrytown, NY; they meet in the plush lounges of clubs like the Links and Knickerbocker, and they make their plans in gatherings of groups like the Council on Foreign Relations. Their news is printed in The Wall Street Journal and Fortune Magazine and they use a language spiked with Monopoly game phrases which is more obscure than the language of any youth culture.[11]

An epilog followed the article, pounding the message home.

> You are all bombers – every one of you who stays in his place, who keeps shellinout/sellinout/paying for the Amerikan nightmare, who doesn't care enough to stop the world bullshit. Did Marine Midland cry out in pain? Does Chase Manhattan mourn the seared and shriveled corpse of its only child? No, no – it wasn't you this time, it couldn't have been you Mr. ABM [American Business Man], big fat earlymorning B52 cocksucker, it wasn't your style. These bombs castrated your property, not your children, and they did something you've never done... they gave fair warning.[12]

Dave Hughey spoke on the mixture of fear and excitement that was swelling in the movement during a speech he gave shortly before going to prison.

A lot of people in the movement are really scared because of what's been happening in the last few months. They're afraid that the actions of the Weathermen and the things that have been going off around the city will escalate the repression and lead to the destruction of the movement the way it is. The problem with the movement is that it is afraid to let go of itself.

One of the functions of any repressive society is that it makes people hold on to things the way they are. For this fucking system here to survive it's absolutely necessary that people hold on to their jobs, their private homes, private cars, private bodies; that men hold on to their domination over women, and women to their submission to men; that whites hold on to their white skin privilege. But most important: that people hold on to the definition of life that this system has given them. Namely that life is that 70 or 80 years after which you die a natural death. So that an 80 year old man who lives 80 years of boredom but dies a natural death is said to have lived a full life. But if an 18 year old kid dies a violent death, that's considered tragic.

As long as people hold on to that definition of life obviously no one is going to challenge the existing order. Because challenging the existing order means putting that which they call life on the line and probably losing it in the process.

So for this movement of resistance and protection to join the revolution, it has to start letting go of some of its institutions and the whole way it defines reality. Our little individual consciousnesses whose main concern is to be protected and to stay alive have to start giving way to a broader consciousness, a collective consciousness and a cosmic consciousness where the individual rather than constantly escaping from life and death and trembling at the slightest signs of repression – lets go and flows into life and into death. And in the context of repressive Amerika this flow into life and death amounts to a very deep and strong desire to fight.[13]

THE INEVITABLE
DIRECTION OF LIFE

In one of his first letters from jail, Sam described, "A mood of despondency I'm not proud of," admitting, "My prevailing mood must be called despair." The extremity of his new circumstances brought self-doubt and an overpowering depression.

"Here I'm stuck with the overwhelming insanity of public opinion and taste without relief! I don't know how long I'll be able to take prison life… Mostly, now I feel whatever I may have hoped to accomplish was simply a waste. Just one more nut who freaked out and took an O.D. or climbed up a tower and fruitlessly gunned down everything in sight… At first the shock of the arrest and the feeling of a common enemy made me groove on my cellmates, but after a while I began to see so painfully the pettiness and hatred that is their preferred makeup. Telling myself these are my fellow creatures just doesn't help for long. I'm not Christ though I might think so sometimes… I don't think I'm strong enough. I think sometimes I have much love for some people and beliefs but I also know that my response to my environment is that of a pragmatic animal."[1]

The Federal House of Detention on West Street in New York City was the first place Sam was held while his case was pending. In a fight with seven white inmates over a game of cards, Sam was badly beaten. All he could do to defend himself was hold onto the prison bars and kick wildly with his legs.

After the fight, he was moved to a cell by himself, and then to a Muslim dominated tier at their request. The Muslims were curious about Sam, and Sam was impressed enough by them to become a vegetarian. His French cellmate, who couldn't speak English, called him "Boom Boom." These things amused him momentarily but his spirits remained low.

After over two months in jail, Sam wrote about how seeing Jane, Dave and their supporters in the courtroom helped pick him up.

"I'm preparing for the worst. When I say that, I can really mean it now. I'm much stronger. The court scenes with all the folks behind us – I can feel the strength of our numbers and determination swelling in my body." [2]

Locked behind bars, Sam began to study, which he rarely

did on the streets, "Reading solid revolutionary thought really helps pull my head together," he wrote, "Without it I can see myself hopelessly falling into the incredible convict mentality of pettiness and stupid mind-destroying thinking about what hacks [guards] to beware of or how much commissary I have left this month."[3]

"The irony of the Amerikan prison system is that it is rehabilitating. Of course for just the opposite reasons its promoters endorse. For the first time since I was a small boy I have no money and no keys in my pockets. You can't imagine the rehabilitating effect of that! From the Muslims I am learning to fast and control my own body. From reading Thoreau and some eastern teachings I can live on much less than even prison allows. I drive my body to extreme exercises until my temples pound. And I am tripping all the time. Not with the frenzy of acid but with the confidence of my liberation from superficialities."[4]

"I knew that as deep as Sam's moods of despair might be he had far too much inner strength to be broken by prison." Jane saw Sam comforted by "the company of other political prisoners, a sign of growing awareness among the inmates, [and] indications that alone as he was he was not totally helpless when he had other human beings around him.[5]

After about four months at West Street, a considerable change could be seen in Sam's outlook. While it was a constant internal struggle, in his letters Sam was sounding more and more like the freedom fighter his friends and supporters knew him to be.

"I am beginning to know the meaning of revolution. It is the desire for ecstasy and I think only desperation can produce it. Those who are willing to yield every last privilege, who drive themselves to the limits of desperation, will make the revolution... what we want is salvation from a meaningless annihilation. Not to be cremated for Coca Cola and plastic flags waving in simulation on the moon. To want that today in Amerika is to be very desperate."[6]

"Only the escalation of action to the point where our situation equals our philosophical desperation will bring whites into the revolution as committed as the others have to be to merely survive."[7]

"If you've been following the papers you know they've been linking me and others to all the shit [political bombing surge in New York and across the U.S.] that's been going down recently... apparently there is now an official, revolutionary underground in the mother country and folks are getting things together at last. It means times will get rougher and tougher from both sides, but that's what this country's needed for many years."[8]

While awaiting trial at West Street, Sam tried to escape twice. That first winter he drew up plans for blasting through the prison walls with dynamite, but the plans were discovered in a shakedown of his cell. At a court date the following March, Sam overpowered a guard, tied his hands with his belt and made a run for it, but was stopped at gunpoint just before reaching the street. After that, Sam was transferred to The Tombs, considered more secure, and infamous for overcrowding and brutality.

The Tombs is designed like a well with balconies circling each floor and a platform in the middle called 'The Bridge.' Dozens of men died each year there from fights, suicides, and beatings from guards that were often staged on The Bridge as an example for the rest of the prisoners.

Sam responded to his new surroundings at The Tombs, writing, "If folks outside could see the conditions under which Amerika forces its misfits to exist I'm sure many would be able to realize the brutal indifference that exists all the way up thru the system."[9]

"Things are very tense here. The hacks act with impunity. I have previously underestimated their willingness to use brutality," he wrote shortly after his arrival, "I don't know what recourse we prisoners have of dealing with them. The inmates are too frightened or untrusting of each other to form alliances. The hacks demand and get instant obedience and they expect a good attitude as well. Dignity is a bourgeois luxury here; survival is where most of us are at."[10]

Yet somehow, Sam found a way to thrive in these

conditions.

"I think the combination of age and a greater coming together is responsible for the speed of the passing time. It's six months now and I can tell you truthfully few periods in my life have passed as quickly. I am in excellent physical and emotional health. There are doubtless subtle surprises ahead but I feel secure and ready. As lovers will contrast their emotions in times of crisis so am I dealing with my environment. In the indifferent brutality, the incessant noise, the experimental chemistry of food, the ravings of lost hysterical men I can act with clarity and meaning. I am deliberate – sometimes even calculating – seldom employing histrionics except as a test of the reactions of others. I read much, exercise, talk to guards & inmates, feeling for the inevitable direction of my life."[11]

At The Tombs, Sam met Herbert X Blyden, a Black Panther who got a concussion from a beating on The Bridge for organizing prisoners. He also met Carlos Feliciano of the struggle for Puerto Rican independence, two Chinese revolutionaries, and Weatherman Lee Wood. These people helped Sam further pull himself out of the depression that consumed him at West Street, in spite of the harsh reality of prison life at The Tombs.

After his sentencing, Sam was moved to a cell by himself, which was extremely rare at the notoriously overcrowded Tombs. He wasn't let out of his cell except for legal visits and showers twice a week. When he showered he was under a captain's guard, and a guard sat within ten feet of his cell refusing to turn the light off throughout each night.

Sam also found out that they were going to have him do state time instead of federal. It was common knowledge among prisoners that state time was more brutal and allowed fewer privileges than federal, but as Sam saw it, jail was jail.[12]

Sing Sing was used as a temporary holding facility for recently sentenced convicts until they were assigned more permanent prisons. Sam was moved there after his sentencing and was immediately segregated for shaving his head bald in protest of the prison's beard and hair regulations.

"I was let into population on Friday," Sam wrote of his

arrival at Sing Sing, "Got some sun, a little exercise… and with the relative freedom of movement, I can feel my body shake out the kinks of nine months lock up… I fondled one of the many cats on the grounds today. The contact of a living being responding to my touch blew my mind."[13]

Inspired by an uprising at The Tombs, Sam began taking steps towards organizing within prison walls, writing that he was, "even more convinced that good political mileage can be had from exploiting liberal hypocrisy toward the prison system. While I am not overly enthusiastic regarding my own participation in this particular matter, if I can be used to any advantage for the forces of social change I will feel much less oppressed by this environment."[14]

Sam fought to stay at Sing Sing because it was closer to New York City, where his visitors would be coming from, but in less than two months he was transferred 350 miles outside New York City to Attica.[15]

"I'm being transferred tomorrow to the big A. It's about 60 miles east of Buffalo I think… Attica does not have a good reputation among inmates but I am in omnia parratus. [in all things prepared]… If you are denied permission to visit me or do not hear from me for more than five or six weeks it will mean I have been boxed – not an uncommon occurrence if one shows signs of wearying of saying sieg heil."

THE EYE OF A HURRICANE

"Get a lawyer," Sam wrote in his first letter from Attica. "I intend to fight before going insane."[1]

"I'm becoming somewhat acclimated now," he affirmed a month later, "and though I lack the double Y chromosome factor of most of my neighbors, I have managed to effect a significantly belligerent aspect to gain, if not the respect, at least the acquiescence of my fellow felons."[2]

"Sam's sincerity impresses me but also scares me," prisoner Bill Coons wrote in his diary when he saw Sam arrive at Attica.[3]

"I won't tread on him," Coons said, "possibly because he's a big guy, over six feet, lanky, loose-limbed, and a full set of calluses on his knuckles from practicing karate against brick and stone jailhouse walls. A heavy dude, this one."[4]

"Sam's a swell guy." Coons wrote after getting to know him better, "Give you the shirt off his back, but he won't wear the right one to mess hall. His war on petty regulations has gotten him two keep-locks thus far... You couldn't trust him alone in the halls; he might rewire the joint and blow it up. That would cause embarrassments when Albany came around."[5]

So far, Sam was surviving prison life. He occasionally found people inside who he could rap politics with and was even considering legal maneuvers aimed at prison reform, but still he felt alienated from the general prison population.

As a revolutionary, Sam saw prisoners as victims of oppressive circumstances that exist within an unjust society, but he had a hard time dealing with the lack of political awareness in most prisoners. Sam was used to the consciousness and freedom of his life on the outside and the contrast of life behind bars made him feel alone and defensive. He often found himself at battle with the prison authorities. Now that he was at Attica, conflict between Sam and the prison guards and administration would only increase.

"I'm in keep-lock for the third time in as many months," Sam wrote at Christmastime, 1970. "This will be a 10-day stretch, maybe more... The 'food' that's passed through the door I relay on to the weird creatures who gather on the windowsill... It's for sure they couldn't survive without the inmates feeding them."[6]

THE EYE OF A HURRICANE

"My health is good and my spirit more afloat than a few months ago," Sam reported in late January, 1971. "There's no indoor recreation here and the weather now prohibits the yard. So, being locked up I've been reading a lot... I do want to prepare a lawsuit to test their stupid brutal regulations... We really can't be optimistic. But it will be a way to make people more conscious of what's going on behind the wall. Those of us who haven't made a life for ourselves inside feel so incredibly cut off. No matter how accurately I could describe it, I don't think you can realize the total isolation of prison life. Each day is exactly like the one before and one has no sense of the immediacy of the revolution in the world... In here one deals only with unrelieved violent male tension. Very un-conductive to spreading seeds and growing plants."[7]

Attica wasn't coming off as the kind of place receptive to revolutionary organizing, so even when Sam wasn't in keep-lock he often kept to his cell studying, doing yoga and feeding the birds. But it was against his nature not to get with the people around him and organize some kind of action against the brutality they were suffering. It wasn't long before Sam was becoming unsatisfied with simply surviving prison.

"It seems to me that the trouble with yoga is that you can get so spaced out you don't care about things like justice or injustice. You have to separate yourself so much from your fellows. I don't think you can have inner peace without outer peace too."[8]

"I've read an article recently about migrating geese; why they fly in that V formation and keep honking. It seems the formation creates a semi-vacuum by the large air movement making it possible to fly long distances without tiring. They honk because they are rooting, cajoling, scolding each other to keep up and keep pumping so the group can make it. Yeah. Honk! Honk!"[9]

"There is no individual change without social change, and there is no social change without political revolution," Sam wrote in March. "Those who are frightened by the cataclysm political revolution presents or who fear the power of repressive status quo have the choice of either being swept under by the maelstrom of social upheaval or using their acumen (gleamed from the suffering of others) to guide us to an understanding of our present political reality so that we may pass to our next evolutionary stage, unforeseeable from our present, narrow, class perspective... The unavoidable conclusion that I arrive at is that I was not born in a vacuum; that I see my reflection in many, many faces. Now, it follows that if I am a sociological phenomenon and I suffer a sociological disease I must have a sociological prognosis. It's here that our viewpoints part. You want to care for each tender shoot while (seemingly) not acknowledging the entire forest is violently aflame. I am presently seeking answers that may tell us whether to put out the fire and repair what we can or help the fire along and hope its end will leave the soil fertile enough to grow anew."[10]

Mob hitman Joseph "Mad Dog" Sullivan was the first ever to escape from Attica in April 1971, infuriating guards and inspiring prisoners like Sam who referred to the escape as, "the great man Sullivan and that Good Friday morn." In the same letter Sam wrote, "There are indications that the hacks are engaging in overt terrorism for a change. Conflicting reports have emerged but something's up for sure."[11]

The combination of Sullivan's escape with the resulting increase in brutality was it for Sam. If he saw oppression on the outside that left him no choice but to fight, he would be fighting in prison as well.

"The Mickey Mouse bullshit they pull on individuals will fall away once we successfully attack the fundamental question of prisoners' rights... Here are some of the things they've busted me for: Walking with hands in pockets; Refusing to go to the mess hall because I wasn't hungry; Refusal to line up according to height; Wearing a white shirt rather than grey to tribunal proceedings; Wearing a sweatshirt to the mess hall; Taking a day off from the 7-day work week in the mess hall... I'm not sure of the exact figure but I've accumulated something around 20 days keep-lock so far... Most of us have had difficulty with oldliners; those pigs who can't get used to not being able to bust heads when somebody doesn't jump when they belch... There are many men here who have either been victim or witness to systematic mistreatment...

THE EYE OF A HURRICANE

We do not have the right to petition among ourselves and we have very adumbrated [obscured] rights to assembly. We are left with nothing except riots to bring our plight before the public. The authorities are very frightened of publicity. They enforce barbaric regulations that 18th century Italians would be ashamed of. Their experience has been: every exposure has proved costly... The parole system must be attacked. Most men in prison are violators. The conditions of parole are so degrading that many men stay in prison and max out... When we are in the yard or mess hall they shake down our cells... If prisoners are obligated to work, the state should be obligated to pay comparable street salaries... As far as rehabilitation is concerned, some of the chief officers have openly admitted to me they don't believe in it. The physical aspect of the education plant here at Attica cannot accommodate more than 1/10 of the inmate population. Many of the men come from NYC and their families simply cannot afford to visit. Nor are they likely to find lodging once they get here... The list is endless: conjugal visits, less pork in the diet, access to viewing TV, Puerto Rican recognition, guards representative of the ethnic population (there are no, repeat no black guards at Attica and one, count him, one Puerto Rican)."[12]

In mid-May, Sam filed a report with his lawyers documenting abuses he was suffering and his actions in protest. He drafted two more documents, titled "History of the Attica Strike" and "An Anatomy of the Laundry," to be circulated among prisoners and outside supporters to organize within Attica's walls.

Report

Since December 1970, I have been trying to get assigned as a C Block porter. I was told by other inmates that if I worked a while in the mess hall I would probably get it. Although the mess hall work is long hard hours and 7 days per week, you lock in C Block and that's where you have to be to get a C Block porter assignment. On March 10, I moved to C Block assigned to the mess hall. I worked hard and cooperated in every way, without incident or report until April 30. When I was returning from work at 5:30 I stopped to chat briefly with a friend who locks a few doors away. Virtually all inmates do this every night until the officer on duty rings the bell to lock in.

As I prepared to leave for work the next morning I found I was keep-locked. This was Saturday May 1. Since the disciplinary tribunal does not meet on weekends I had to wait until Monday to know the charges against me. The charges read to me in court Monday said I refused to lock in when told by the officer on duty and also that I made a contemptuous gesture to the officer. I of course denied the charge. The charge was signed by officer Brown. The chief officer Mulrooney then asked me who locked in 36-5 cell, that I felt compelled to speak to every night. I said I didn't see how that was relevant. Mulrooney said he didn't care what I thought was relevant and insisted I answer his question. I said if he wanted to know so badly he could easily look it up. He then sentenced me to five days keep-lock with two days served.

On Wednesday May 5, I was released and reported back to mess hall. The next day I was told to pack up, I was moving. I asked where to and was told one flight downstairs to the C Block porters company. Naturally I was glad. I reported to work after moving my things and was told I was an extra, that I would be assigned in a few days.

On Tuesday May 11, I was called in to the desk and told I was moving to D Block to be assigned to the State shop (where incoming inmates are fitted for clothing). Normally you are not moved from one block to another unless you request it. I protested I had made no request to move and did not want to move. The officers said they would have to move me if I refused. They suggested I lock in at my new location and would go to court the next day. I did. At court the chief officer said he didn't know why I was moved and that I should put in a request to see the Deputy Warden and he could explain. He further suggested I report to work as assigned to avoid further difficulties. I did as instructed. The next day, Thursday May 13, I was called to the administration block for an interview with Mr. Pheil, the Assistant Deputy Warden. I asked him why I was moved. He replied Mr. Mancusi had instructed it, that I was a security risk and could better be supervised in D block. I asked in what way was D Block more secure than C Block. He replied he was only following orders and if I wanted to see the warden I should put in an interview request.

I returned to my cell and informed the officer on duty I was refusing any further cooperation. I was immediately keep-locked. On the next morning, Friday, May 14, I appeared once more before the disciplinary tribunal. I told them I was refusing any further assignment until either I spoke with my attorney or they restored my former assignment as C Block porter. They said the warden had ordered the change and they had not the power to move me back. They gave me 7 days keep-lock for refusing work.[13]

History of the Attica Strike

Sometime in the spring of 1970, a small group of inmates in B Block drew up a petition asking for higher wages and lower commissary prices. (B Block, with 500 inmates is immediately attached to the industrial plant. Most of those who lock in B work in the metal shop, producing state-used material, sold to other state institutions.) The petitioners gathered around 125 names on the petition and presented it to Warden Mancusi. The administration selected from the list of names those they thought were responsible and immediately "boxed" them (put in punitive segregation). Subsequently, most of B Block locked their doors and refused to work. The administration had all of B Block locked in and kept it locked for about two weeks. Most of the "leaders" who had been boxed were shipped out to other institutions. Things returned to normal with the administration saying it was considering some salary changes (and they reduced commissary immediately).

In the fall, a directive from Albany came listing the various jobs and grouping them, attaching a wage scale to each group. All salaries were raised considerably, e.g.; metal shop workers jumped from 15¢-55¢/day to $1.00/day; school instructors from 15¢-55¢ to 85¢/day; etc.

Since the initial commissary price drop, prices have been raised monthly to a point now where every item has increased over the original price prior to the reduction. Sometimes this had been done by changing the unit price, e.g., prior to the strike, a 20 oz. jar of wheat germ cost 54¢, presently, a 12 oz. jar of wheat germ costs 48¢.[14]

An Anatomy of the Laundry

Because of the Pig-sanctioned Right to capitalize on the needs of other inmates, and the accompanying fear of losing their lucrative Jobs, our brothers who work in the Laundry have become docile slaves, House-Niggers, and therefore, an impediment to our Liberation.

These Laundry slaves, who, for the most part, are some well-meaning and intelligent individuals, have been so thoroughly

THE EYE OF A HURRICANE

indoctrinated and duped by this Dog-eat-Dog system that they don't even realize that they have become House-Niggers and instruments of their own oppression.

How does the Pig exploit the Laundry slave? How does the Pig profit? Like so: The average wage of a unionized Dry Laundry Worker on the outside is $3.50 per hour, whereas, the average wage of a Laundry slave here is 25¢ per day; an outside unionized worker would earn $10.50 for the same work. Projected to a monthly basis, the slave gets $5.50, while an outsider gets $231.00. There are 40 slaves in the Laundry for a monthly payroll of $220.00. If the State were forced to pay union wages, the payroll would be $9,240.00. Yearly, it's $2,640.00 as compared to $110,880.00 (Dig). Our active support of this saves the State $108,240.00 annually.

HOW?

The slaves are allowed three Laundry contracts at one carton ($33.50) per month. So the slave's real salary is $10.50 per month, plus the $5.50. Who pays this? WE DO! We pay the slave $3.50 for four workdays a month, work which he completes in no time at all. The Pig pays the slave $5.00 for 22 days of hard work! Thus, the State gets 18 more days of labor than we do, for our $3.50, and the State only pays the slave $1.50 more. Now, I ask you, is that ignorant slave with the crease in his pants slick, or is the Pig slick? The Pig gets the cash saving, the labor, and the wages paid to the slave as soon as the Commissary opens.

So, you see Brother-Man, we have the power to stop this. No Riots or Violence but just refusing to cooperate in maintaining our own misery just because we want a crease in our pants and don't want to wash our own dirty underwear.

Yes, let's force the Pig to bring in those unionized laundries and pay that $110,880.00 a year to run the laundry. By saving $3.50, we can cost him $110,880.00 that he can't afford.

Brother-Man, now is the time to act!

STOP PAYING!

JUST HOLD BACK AND MAKE THIS COOKIE CRUMBLE!!!!!!

PEACE & POWER

YOUR (SLAVE) LAUNDRY MAN

RIGHT ON!!!!! RIGHT ON!!!!! RIGHT ON!!!!!

Abuses in Attica only kept getting worse, and about a third of his time there Sam was in keep-lock.[15] "They're fucking with my mail, books, and visiting rights. And I'm practicing anal distension to be prepared."[16]

"I have been moved to observation (box), where all my possessions were taken and are being returned piecemeal. At the assistant superintendent hearing I was sentenced to 30 days in the box and 15 days lost good time. I have no intention of returning to work. That will mean no good time and probably no parole in addition to remaining boxed for the remainder of the sentence."[17]

"On Wednesday, May 19, 1971, I was called for an interview with F.B.I. agents Biard & Davidson. They told me what they wanted to talk to me about and read off the warning of rights. They then asked if I would speak to them and I said I would have to speak to my lawyer first. They asked me if I would answer questions regarding the Milwaukee Federal building explosion in Sept. '69. They then asked if I would answer questions concerning the whereabouts of certain fugitives. After I said I would have to speak to my lawyer I asked to see the pictures in front of him (Biard). He showed me pix of the four accused of the Wisconsin Univ. Math Center and pix of Jane and Pat Swinton. He asked if I knew any of them and I said I'd have to speak with my lawyer. I then left the room."[18]

"They've taken my earphones away – again for not folding my arms. Each time I leave the cell for shower, shave, meet the panel, I get another report for not folding arms. First they took away exercise yard, now earphones. Next it will be light bulb and newspaper and books. I've decided not to leave my cell anymore which means they'll drag me I guess. Can you get these motherfuckers off my back?" Sam pleaded with his lawyers, "Try Oswald or Field, the appeals court head. Anybody!"[19]

"Sam will handle himself wherever he is," prisoner Bill Coons wrote when he noticed Sam was being moved all over the prison. "His only problem is with the hacks. He doesn't really hate them much, but the system puts them directly in his way. Otherwise they'd probably both be glad to ignore each other."[20]

On June 20, 1971, Sam filed a complaint himself with New York State Commissioner of Corrections, Russell Oswald.

Dear Mr. Oswald,

I am in punitive segregation at Attica prison.

Chronology of events:

May 7: Moved without request from C Block porter to D Block State Shop.

May 10: Interview with Mr. Pfiel to ascertain why I was moved. He said the Warden thinks I am better supervised in D Block. I refused to work until restored to C Block.

May 12: Sentenced to 8 days keep-lock.

May 21: Again refuse to work.

May 22: Sentenced to keep-lock pending interview with Deputy Warden.

June 4: Mr. Vincent sentences me to 30 days in punitive segregation with 15 days lost time.

June 15: When returning from exercise yard I am told to fold my arms (for the first time). I refuse.

June 11 [sic.]: Sentenced to "14 days keep-lock or until he conforms to rules."

I want to be restored to my former position as C Block porter and my lost time returned to me. If I am to remain in punitive segregation I want exercise privileges.

Sam Melville
#26124"[21]

While refusing to work Sam kept studying in his cell, but now he applied his studies differently. He began relating the revolution to the struggles of prison life and exposing the movement on the outside to the awareness that was building behind bars.

"Not only might the oppressed not have the power to enforce their will, but in common with most individuals they do not evaluate society on the basis of its conformity to the radical's abstract standard of justice. Rather, they act and evaluate on the basis of perceived self-interest, and of value and belief patterns promoted by the ruling class to secure social harmony and integration... A radical consciousness will spread... only insofar as it responds to their basic needs, and will effect revolution only insofar as it is close to the sources of economic power."[22]

"To any impartial observer, the primary contradiction today is not between the workers and the bourgeoisie; it's not between the neo-colonialist and the 3rd world; the primary contradiction has at last been reduced to the simplest terms: between the armed and the unarmed. We've had victories. But some of the flock are getting too fat to fly long distances. And their honking sounds gurgled. And the dark erythric fluid dripping from their beaks makes it disconcerting to embrace them."[23]

Sam was asked by publisher Ramparts to review a book on the Weathermen and, even though the prison authorities never allowed the book in, he was invigorated with a renewed sense of having a place in the struggle.

"I really enjoy the visits," Sam wrote to a friend in July. "They pull me from these ruts of Times-Study-Headstands that I tend to ossify in. As I study and learn, the visits get so much more meaningful. I shed more and more of the shroud of incantation I use to hide ignorance. Each return to the cell after a visit makes me attack this ignorance with greater determination."[24]

By the end of July, the "History of the Attica Strike"

THE EYE OF A HURRICANE

and "An Anatomy of the Laundry" documents had evolved into a larger project. Sam began secretly publishing a hand-written carbon-copied newsletter, called *The Iced Pig*, that was distributed by hand from prisoner to prisoner.

THE ICED PIG
Number 1
Attica Newsletter

Power Brothers! Poder Hermanos!
This is the first issue of what will be a continuing project. A project that will help to bring each other to an understanding of our place and the role of neo-fascist Amerika and the Amerikan Auschwitz known as Attica.
Of primary importance is the coming awareness of ourselves as political prisoners. No matter how heinous the "crime" you have been convicted of, no matter how many people you offed, drugs you pushed, whores you ran, places you robbed, you are a political prisoner just as much as Angela [Angela Davis, an internationally known U.S. political prisoner in 1971]. Every act has a cause and effect. The cause of your crime is that you found yourself in a society that offered no prospects for a life of fulfillment and sharing with your brothers and sisters. A society where you were taught to compete and beat the guy next to you because if you didn't, he'd beat you. A society whose every facet and angle is thoroughly controlled by the Pigdogs of the corporation giants of Amerika. The apparent effect of your "crime" is that now you find yourself locked behind tons of steel and concrete, completely brutalized, cut off from any warmth and affection. But the real effect is that you have become waste material to Amerika's ruling class. By your "crime" you have shown

89

MAD BOMBER MELVILLE

Amerika's bosses that you can't cooperate in the "free enterprise system." That is to say, you won't accept $100 a week for breaking your balls while some fat-assed capitalist drives around in the Mercedes you paid for. By your "crime" you were only doing in a crude way what the Rockefellers and Fords have been doing since they stole this country from the Indians 200 years ago.

Yes brothers, in every sense of the word you are political prisoners. And now we owe it to ourselves and the great masses of struggling humanity, to teach ourselves the truth of Amerika's myth. To forge ourselves into dedicated cadres committed to the construction of a society that will serve the needs of the people and make us into whole human beings at last.

Future issues of The Iced Pig will discuss strategy and tactics of our role in the coming revolution. Every individual's participation is necessary if we are to continue to grow. Make your contribution known by joining the political rap sessions in your yard.[25]

By late July, Sam wrote of changes at Attica, "We've gathered a coterie of young freaks and we rap politics a lot. The place is beginning to crawl with 20yearoldnamvets busted for dope out of Rochester and Buffalo."[26]

At that time he also filed a complaint signed by fifteen prisoner witnesses stating, "On Tuesday, July 27, 1971, officer Boyle of D Block made his way through the corridor near C Block, shoving and knocking several inmates of 5 and 2 company who were returning from the mess hall. Mr. Boyle had ample room to make his way without molesting others."[27]

Two weeks later he wrote of its futility, "We have heard nothing of our complaint about pig Boyle except to note that the rules about staying in line and talking in the corridor are being more strictly enforced."[28]

By early August 1971, Sam was seeking organizing help

90

from an attorney beyond filing legal motions for prison reform, "A new Manifesto is currently being prepared... We are in need of a lawyer who can devote a significant part of his or her time to helping us with technicalities, keeping our stuff moving in the courts and meeting with us once a month for progress reports and important other things... we have 5 or 7 people (myself included) who would be listed as clients of this lawyer so hopefully we could all meet together – something we cannot do otherwise."[29]

"Lists of demands have been circulating around the blocks, seeking general inmate approval," prisoner Bill Coons wrote in his diary. "Sam probably did some, but he's not the only one."[30]

In a plea with an attorney who was considering helping Sam and the others organizing under the Attica Anti-Depression League, Sam wrote this letter.

Oh it's true there have been changes: in the year I've been at Attica they've added a civilian to the disciplinary tribunal; tepid water pitchers now adorn the mess hall tables; basketball courts have been built (completely constructed, designed and financed by the inmates); lights out is now at 11 rather than 10 p.m. It's true we can gather in groups greater than three without being gassed or clubbed. It's true penalties involving one's visiting rights have ceased. Wages have been raised from 10¢ to 25¢ a day (!) (countered by an approximately 30% per unit rise in commissary prices)... I'm thinking hard for more, but that's it. Not a mill for educational facilities or training programs and equipment; nothing about censorship of mail; nothing about literature relating to our lives being made available to us; nothing about due process in disciplinary proceedings; nothing about institutional racism where the 20% white population occupy 100% of the privileged jobs and influence other appointments and activities;

where blacks number 60% and Puerto Ricans 20% of the population yet are supervised totally by incredibly stupid local farmboy honkey pigs.

I won't go into the Mickey Mouse bullshit like attire, hair lengths, talking in the corridor, lining up by height, etc., etc.; those types of things are stopped when the more important essentials of prison life are changed. Nor do I have the space and understanding yet to go into parole violation procedure or terms of so-called 'conditional release.' Nor will I dwell on the very lucrative capitalist enterprise prison represents to the state and a few Tweedish motherfuckers at the top. Health facilities are reminiscent of 1942 Buchenwald... Accordingly, the death rate at Attica is 2.2 per month for a population of just under 2000.

The Attica Anti-Depression League... has drawn up and submitted a list of over 20 demands... Men who are politically aware and potential leaders are shuffled frequently and isolated from each other. For instance, the only contact we in A Block have with the brothers in B Block is furtive note-passing in religious services. Consequently, we are thinking now in terms of getting one lawyer assigned to five or eight men as representatives from the different blocks just so we can get a chance to meet regularly and clear up our mutual thinking. This lawyer would come up regularly each month for about three hours – making progress reports, helping with technical shit in writs – but basically to give us inmates a chance to knock our heads together."[31]

In early August, the second issue of Sam's newsletter surfaced.

THE ICED PIG
Number 2

THE EYE OF A HURRICANE

Attica Newsletter

In the aftermath of newspaper articles unfavorable to prison, Mancusi & company are coming out of their old pig bag again. With their muscle and fascist clubs they are trying to head off the growing tendency, both inside and outside the wall, to treat us as something more than dogs. Corridor rules about lining up, no talking, etc., as well as bullshit mess hall regulations are all being strictly enforced now. All the old Mickey Mouse bullshit hasn't gotten a play in the newspapers so the pig is using them to come down on us. The aim of this harassment is clear: they're trying to intimidate us into silence; into crawling meekly back to our cells and not raising a cry of protest. We must not let this happen! We must make our voices heard.

There are several things we can do – all of which are legal:

(1) Every man can write a brief letter requesting an interview with his hometown newspaper. If the pigs don't let it out, so much the better. Save the rejected letter and the written reason for not being able to send it. This is evidence for when we have to bring class action.

(2) Write your congressman (sealed letters) stating the dog-like treatment you are receiving as a result of change being forced upon the prison.

(3) Check around the yard for feeling about a one-day work stoppage – not a strike – just a brief vacation to dramatize our conditions to the outside.

We must not sit mute! The opportunity to raise our conditions to a level to produce meaningful understanding of our role in society is very near. If we let it slip through our hands, the

prison system will fall back into the 18th century
again. Make your voices heard![32]

"I can't tell you what a change has come over the brothers
in Attica," Sam wrote in August to a brother who had been
released. "So much more awareness and growing consciousness
of themselves as revolutionaries. Reading, questioning, rapping
all the time. Still bigotry and racism, black, white and brown, but
you can feel it beginning to crumble in the knowledge so many
are gaining that we must build solidarity against our common
oppressor – the system of exploitation of each other and alienation
from each other. Since you left, a group has formed under the
title of the Anti-Depression League, as yet a small group trying
to create an alliance between all the various factions – Panthers,
Young Lords, white radicals, Five Percenters, Orthodox Muslims,
etc. Not an easy task as you well know. Among the problems we
face is how to form revolutionary awareness relating to our prison
condition… There's only one revolutionary change as far as the
prison system in Amerika is concerned. But until the day comes
when enough of our brothers and sisters realize what that one
revolutionary change is, we must always be certain our demands
will exceed what the pigs are able to grant."[33]

One prisoner said that during the changes sweeping
Attica, "Sam was a prince of war among imprisoned fighters.
To blacks he was that missing proof that white revolutionaries
deserve black respect. To whites he was like a shield against their
own privilege-fed cowardice. He made whites believe in their
own courage just by the way he walked down the halls or talked
to the really pig hacks."[34]

"Sam turned the inmates' respect into support, and then
he turned this support into power. As the inmates' support for Sam
grew, the hacks became somewhat less willing to push him around.
And the more the hacks backed off, the harder Sam pushed… And
because he gave the guards more truck, the inmates respected him
more. It was a spiral of increasing power which Sam consciously
created and maintained."[35]

Things were moving faster and faster. All signs showed
that Attica was a powder keg ready to explode but the authorities

only responded with more repression.

"Presently in keep-lock (14 days) for demanding human treatment. The pigs say I was creating a disturbance in the mess hall. Political people in at least three blocks have been busted this week for petty shit."[36]

By the end of the month Sam had published the third issue of his newsletter.

THE ICED PIG
Number 3
Attica Newsletter

You are beautiful brothers! Strength and Solidarity are the greatest weapons to gain dignity. Strength and Solidarity is what you showed on the 27th. As if one man, there was silence and fasting at the noon mess in memory of our revolutionary brother George Jackson. Many Brothers wore black armbands defying the pigs' barbaric dress code. One brother in A Block was locked up behind it but the head pig cut him loose.

You scored two other victories last week too: (1) Behind our more than 500 signature petition, the institution is now providing the prizes for the Labor Day events – no more from our pockets. (2) A new list on the bulletin board shows that now we can read a broader range of literature. These are very small victories but they demonstrate the growing feeling of unity and this means strength. And strength is the road to dignity.

Some of the ruling class media tried to show a racist motive behind the killings of the two white prisoners at San Q but nobody's going for it. These two were lackey attendants and you don't get to attendant status without wiping the man's ass.

MAD BOMBER MELVILLE

> On the day of Jackson's funeral, the
> Weatherpeople bombed 3 offices of the California
> Corrections Dept. Unfortunately, no one was
> hurt. Get it together Weatherfolk![37]

On August 21, 1971, George Jackson was shot to death by guards
at California's San Quentin prison. Jackson was imprisoned on
a one-year-to-life felony sentence after robbing $71 from a gas
station when he was eighteen. During his twelve years in prison,
Jackson became a member of the Black Panther Party, founded
prison organizations and authored two books, Soledad Brother
and Blood in My Eye.

George's fame further grew on August 7, 1970, when
his seventeen-year-old brother, Jonathan Jackson, led a high
profile kidnapping in a Marin County, California courthouse.
The kidnapping aimed to free George, Fleeta Drumgo and John
Clutchette, who were known as the Soledad Brothers for being
charged with the murder of a guard in Soledad Prison. As Jonathan
and his band fled the courthouse with two freed prisoners and the
judge as hostage, the police showered them with bullets. The only
survivor was Jonathan's comrade Ruchell Magee, who received a
life sentence. Angela Davis was accused of being an accomplice
and placed on the F.B.I.'s Most Wanted list, but was eventually
acquitted.

George Jackson's books were very popular, and prisoners
across America considered him a hero. In response to his murder,
Sam helped organize a meal strike at Attica.

"It was the weirdest thing," guard Jack Williams
explained. "They all walked in as usual, divided into two lines
and walked through the serving area. But nobody picked up a tray
or a spoon, and nobody took any food. They just walked through
the line and went to their seats and they sat down. They looked
straight ahead and nobody made a sound. You could have heard
your wristwatch ticking. It was eerie. Then we noticed that almost
all had some black on them – some had cloth armbands, some
had black shoelaces around their arms, others had pieces of black
cloth pinned on them. It scared us, because a thing like that takes
a lot of organization, a lot of solidarity, and we had no idea they

96

were so well organized."[38]

"The lumpen are very excited at the strong display of solidarity exhibited last Friday," Sam wrote. "At the midday meal, not a man ate or spoke – black, white, brown, red. Many wore black armbands. The priest was asked to say a prayer, and after some to-do, did so. No one can remember anything like it here before."[39]

The strike frightened prison authorities and they responded with yet more repression.

"I was down to the disciplinary court two weeks ago and there were more than seventy men waiting for a hearing. The old-timers say it's beginning to look like the old days where you got keep-lock for looking cross-eyed at the pig. They're enforcing the tiniest shit now. I'm finishing a 14-day keep-lock for a small mess hall infraction which is just a reprimand... A hard worker in D Block just got a 60-day box bit for having the manifesto and progressive lit in his cell."[40]

"We have only one other alternative to meet their aggression, and at this time geography is against that – not to mention technology."[41]

"It is true I have much anger, but to say I am angry at the world not only misses the point but casts much doubt on any of the constructive energy my anger has generated... If you want to believe a man who is often angry but nevertheless sometimes possesses a remarkable ear, I tell you we are living in the eye of a hurricane. That the violent and irrepressible winds of change are swirling around us throughout a world that will no longer pay the bill of our government's repine appetite. And that soon the tremors of the last couple of years will be as a sleeping lion lazily swatting a fly with his tail."[42]

"All rules are now strictly enforced," Sam wrote in his last letter from Attica on September 4, 1971, "Attire, haircuts, lining up, not talking, no wearing hats – everything. You're busted for dispensing literature, holding meetings, or staring at pigs. We are treated as dogs. Don't wag your righteous finger at Mancusi and pretend you're shocked. Sue the motherfucker, or better yet shoot him. But for Christ's sake do something."[43]

SEPTEMBER 9 - 13, 1971

9

Five days later, Sam's warnings came true. The cover of the *Buffalo Evening News* headlined, "Attica Inmates Seize Four Cellblocks; 11 Guards Hurt, Others Held Hostage"[1]

The paper traced the origin of the outbreak to an incident the night before where an inmate threw a piece of glass and injured a guard. Breakfast went as usual on the morning of September 9th, but by 9:30 a.m. the prison sirens were sounding. The prison chapel and workshop were set on fire by the prisoners early and continued to burn until about noon. Guard William Quinn suffered serious head injuries in the uprising. He, and ten other prison guards suffering lesser injuries, received medical treatment at nearby hospitals. Guards, assisted by state troopers and sheriff's deputies, were only able to maintain control of the powerhouse, administration buildings and the prison walls, leaving the estimated 1,000 rioting prisoners free range over the rest of the prison. Rebelling prisoners became known as the 'Attica Brothers' to supporters around the country.

"Some of the guards were beaten and stripped by the convicts," the article reported. "Some guards walked out wearing blankets around their waists. Others came out on stretchers."

"They have hostages," a sheriff told reporters, "I don't know how many."

"I've got bad trouble," said Superintendent Vincent R. Mancusi, calling the situation "an emergency."

An unidentified prison guard was quoted in the paper, saying, "The place is blowing up."

The taking of the prison was so well executed that a captain reasoned, "It almost has to be well planned."

175 sheriff's deputies from Buffalo were mobilized along with sheriff's deputies from Genessee County. New York State Governor Rockefeller and State Corrections Commissioner Russell G. Oswald were discussing whether or not to deploy National Guard troops to the prison.

By noon the Attica Brothers sent word that they were willing to negotiate with Oswald and Rockefeller. Oswald was in an airplane on his way to Attica.[2]

A separate article in the paper described what visitors to the prison witnessed that morning.

SEPTEMBER 9 - 13, 1971

"I heard gunshots about 10:30 a.m.," a female visitor commented. "I also saw some guards stripped down, wearing just a blanket coming across the entrance. I saw about three of them. I saw guards cut up with blood over them on stretchers and two walked out with blood on their shirts."[3]

"I heard someone on the loud speaker saying 'suspend visiting because there's trouble inside,'" another visitor told a reporter. "I went outside the prison and waited. I saw smoke and about twenty minutes after that I saw the ambulances take two prisoners."[4]

On Friday, September 10, 1971, the press reported that the Attica Brothers were holding thirty-one guards and four civilian shop foremen as hostages. Rebelling prisoners were now estimated at 1,280, over half the prison population. They were armored with football helmets and masks made of cloth, and carried pipes, homemade knives and baseball bats. On the other side of the wall were 600 troopers and deputies from 14 counties packing teargas grenades, shotguns, AR-15 rifles and Thompson submachine guns. Sharpshooters with .270-caliber rifles and sniper scopes were posted in the highest prison towers.

When helicopters began to hover over D-Yard the Attica Brothers brought hostages out with pillowcases over their heads demanding the choppers ground.

A doctor was allowed into the prisoner-controlled yard to examine the hostages and determined that they'd suffered only very minor scrapes and bruises, and were being treated well.

The papers explained how, on Thursday afternoon, 220 state troopers and 75 sheriff's deputies retook areas of the prison abandoned by the rebelling prisoners who were mostly gathered in D-Yard, the recreation yard for the prisoners locked in Attica's D-Block.

"If somebody on the other side gets killed, well that's the way it's gonna be," a State Police Captain prepped his troops for the retaking. "You're to take no crap from anybody. Don't lose your weapon and don't lose your buddy."[5]

When police advanced, the Attica Brothers held D-Yard but lost control of other parts of the prison.

When Oswald arrived late on Thursday, he made his way to a negotiating table in the rebel-held area of the prison through pools of dirty water, mud and broken glass. Oswald met with prisoners for forty-five minutes and agreed to a temporary truce and "no administrative reprisals."

The Attica Brothers demanded that reporters be at the negotiation tables to bring their voices to the public.

"After we were searched we were marched through the corridor under very tight security to a negotiating area where a table was set up. They even had typewriters there and were waiting for the confrontation," reporters described, "They are very angry and they want certain demands met."[6]

At the first negotiations the Attica Brothers issued five "demands" and fifteen "practical proposals."

> To the people of America,
> The incident that has erupted here at Attica is not a result of the dastardly bushwacking of the two prisoners Sept. 8, 1971 but of the unmitigated oppression wrought by the racist administration network of the prison, throughout the year.
> WE are MEN! We are not beasts and do not intend to be beaten and driven as such. The entire prison population has set forth to change forever the ruthless brutalization and disregard for the lives of the prisoners here and throughout the United States. What has happened here is but the sound before the fury of those who are oppressed.
> We will not compromise on any terms except those that are agreeable to us. We call upon all the conscientious citizens of America to assist us in putting an end to this situation that threatens the life of not only us but of each and every person in the United States as well."[7]

The Fifteen Practical Proposals were a list of prison reforms so basic that they were shocking to many Americans who assumed that conditions inside U.S. prisons were humane.

"Their basic demands are no more radical than decent food, good medical care, adequate recreational opportunities, better rehabilitation programs," wrote a newspaper editorial. "These things ought to have been provided long ago."

The editorial also cited a New York State Committee on Crime and Correction held earlier that year. "It is our firm conviction that any penal system which falls short of affording to its prison inmates the fundamental dignities to which all human beings are entitled demeans our society and threatens its future safety."[8]

In the Five Demands, prisoners insisted that there be a civilian observers' committee to oversee negotiations that consisted of several key political figures on the outside, including members of the Black Panther Party, the Young Lords Party, the Urban League, representatives from radical and mainstream newspapers, attorneys, politicians and others.

The press couldn't say enough about the demands for release and transportation to a non-imperialist country and complete amnesty from reprisals, but there was also a good portion of media coverage of the inhumane prison conditions that sparked the uprising.

"We work under slave conditions here," a prisoner told reporters. "We are paid 30¢ and 40¢ a day. The shops here earn $2 million. Where's that money going?"

Other prisoners told the press about not receiving physicals for nine years, dental treatment that was so neglectful that their teeth rotted out and their mouths were full of pus, guards destroying their law books, degrading treatment at the parole board, failing drug treatment programs, unsanitary conditions, racial discrimination, and other problems. They spoke of being treated like "children" and "animals."

"I have been in jail for ten years," one man said. "This is the worst prison I've ever been in. This is a death house."[9]

"The more you do for the prisoners the more they want," argued a department of corrections employee. "You can't give them everything but they have been led to expect it and when you can't produce, they go on a rampage."[10]

A number of guards took the stance that prison reform would make their jobs harder and more dangerous, adding that, "prisoners all over the country have the idea that society is now on their side."[11]

People came from all around to see for themselves what was happening in the little-known country village, creating a "carnival atmosphere." The draw was so large that a local Lions Club set up a hamburger grill in front of the prison, the Salvation Army set up a canteen and doctors opened up small clinics. A group of young men brought a keg of beer to the roadside and watched the scene unfold for hours.

When a busload of black anti-poverty activists from Buffalo arrived in Attica, the village's Tipperary restaurant put the "Closed" sign on the front door.

"The inmates aren't normal humans like you and I," the wife of a guard explained, "We never committed murder."[12]

At Rockefeller's office in Manhattan, over fifty people gathered with signs reading, "Free the Poor, Jail the Rich" and "Jail Rockefeller." They had a list of twenty-seven demands smuggled out of Attica to present to the Governor but were refused.

"In all concentration camps like these," a spokesperson for the protesters said, "men must stand up for their rights."[13]

"The very fury and the apparent scope of the Attica revolt add powerful reinforcement to the mounting evidence that the nation simply cannot afford any more out-of-sight, out-of-mind indifference to the explosive conditions which breed such outbreaks," a newspaper editorial argued. "The sources of Attica's agony are all too characteristic of the ingredients waiting detonation wherever these explosive ingredients of despair, desperation and rage reach a 'critical mass'... Surely Attica's nightmare should remove any doubt about the urgent need for a national awakening to the changing prisoner population and spreading unrest which make fundamental constructive reforms an imperative necessity."[14]

Rockefeller refused to make the trip to Attica. His staff told reporters, "It might be politically advantageous for the governor to go personally to Attica but he feels he has competent men already on the scene there."[15]

Newspapers reported that William Quinn, the guard most injured in the initial rebellion, remained in serious condition in a Rochester hospital.

On Saturday, September 11, 1971, the news reported that prisoners still controlled all of D-Block, the corridors of A-Block, most of B-Block and the catwalks and main guard tower, called "Times Square," that divided the exercise yards of the different blocks. Six buildings were now reported burned during the first day of the uprising, including the prison school.

Reports of the negotiations focused on "more hostility towards Commissioner Oswald" and a radical leadership emerging from the rebelling prisoners. Frustrated rebels were said to jump onto the negotiating table with the microphone commanding attention. The Attica Brothers were now demanding the dismissal of Superintendent Mancusi, but backed down on the demand for release and transport to a non-imperialist country.

One reporter described the Attica Brothers as having "military-style discipline," writing, "Every place you went… you were surrounded and separated by a line of guards, standing side by side, their arms locked."

"I'm ready to die for this," declared a prisoner. "It's better to die like a man than crawling on your knees."[16]

On his way out from the negotiations, Oswald leaned towards a journalist and whispered, "It's a serious situation. I didn't think we'd get out."[17]

The press was allowed to talk with the hostages, who were being kept in a ring of benches with mattresses covering the ground.

"Just tell everybody we've been treated good," a hostage said. "Tell them we're fine and that they've been feeding us."

"I want you to hear now," a prisoner shouted. "Most of us are sleeping on the bare ground, but you can see for yourself that [the hostages] are all sleeping on mattresses."[18]

Oswald said demands for the minimum wage for prison labor and parole reform were beyond his abilities. A Wyoming

County District Attorney dismissed the possibility of amnesty for rebelling prisoners, "Nobody, not even the Governor himself, nor anybody else, could enjoin responsible authorities from prosecuting cases at law which it is their duty to prosecute."[19]

Supporters of the Attica Brothers in Buffalo chanted, "End Concentration Camps For the Poor; the Rich Get Richer and the Poor Go To Jail" and "Hitler, Oswald, Both the Same; Tear the Prisons Down." They marched down Main Street and passed out mimeographed lists of the Five Demands and the Fifteen Practical Proposals.

Guard William Quinn was still in the hospital in critical condition after having surgery to release pressure in his head. Oswald was now claiming that Quinn was thrown down stairs when the riots broke out.

A cartoon in the *Buffalo Evening News*, titled "Time Bomb," pictured a prison representing "Every U.S. Prison" and a giant bomb sitting on top of it, fuse burning. In the far background was an explosion reading "San Quentin," where George Jackson was killed just weeks earlier. Closer to the foreground was a second explosion, labeled "Attica."[20]

The Sunday, September 12, 1971, *New York Times* reported the death of Guard William Quinn. Officials were now claiming that prisoners threw Quinn out of a second-story cellblock window when the riot broke out Thursday morning.

Until Quinn's death, negotiations seemed to be progressing. Oswald was agreeing to almost all of the demands and the whole country was watching the events unfold through the media. Now that a guard had been killed, an agreement over the amnesty demand was unimaginable.

Oswald had agreed to every demand except amnesty and the firing of Superintendent Mancusi, who the prisoners hated so much that a townsperson said, "If he had set foot inside that courtyard, they would have killed him."[21]

Rockefeller still refused to go to Attica. A secretary of his was sent but didn't take part in the negotiations. Outside the prison a few dozen people gathered and chanted, "Free the Attica Prisoners – Jail Rockefeller."[22]

The observers' committee tried to keep hopes up as they emerged from the prison walls claiming, "there was a good chance this could end" if both sides continued to "bargain in good faith."

"We have assurances that there are no present plans to use force," an observer confirmed. "I hope it continues... I hope the authorities don't precipitate tragedy."[23]

The morning *New York Times* on Monday, September 13, 1971, reported an increase in police forces at Attica and equipment including high-pressure water hoses and a van full of riot helmets.

"I urgently request you to release the hostages unharmed, now," Oswald gave an ultimatum. "Only after these steps are taken am I willing to meet... to discuss any grievances you may have... It is in the interest of all concerned that you now respond affirmatively to this request."[24]

Their answer was to bring eight hostages onto the catwalk with shanks held to their throats.

The committee of observers released an urgent statement saying they were now, "convinced a massacre of prisoners and guards may take place in this institution. For the sake of our common humanity," they pleaded with Governor Rockefeller to, "please go to Attica Prison."[25]

Rockefeller replied, "In view of the fact that the key issue is total amnesty... I do not feel that my personal presence on the site can contribute to a settlement... I do not have the constitutional authority to grant such a demand and I would not even if I had the authority because to do so would undermine the very essence of our free society – the fair and impartial application of the law."[26]

Many others felt that the Governor's presence was needed to give authenticity to negotiations and was the only thing that could end the conflict peacefully.

Black Panther Chairman Bobby Seale, who was a member of the observers' committee, knew something was up when he wasn't allowed back into the prison.

"This morning the Commissioner and his aides would not let me in, saying that if I was not going inside to encourage the prisoners to accept the so-called demands made by the committee, they did not want me. I'm not going to do that... In addition the Commissioner said that full amnesty was nonnegotiable and removal of the Warden at Attica Prison was nonnegotiable. The Black Panther Party position is this: The prisoners have to make their own decision. I will not encourage them to compromise their position."[27]

A reporter predicted that it would soon be "shotgun and teargas time."[28]

At 7:46 a.m. Oswald gave final warning, "I urgently request you to seriously reconsider my earlier appeal that (1) all hostages be released immediately unharmed; and (2) you join with me in restoring order to the facility. I must have your reply to this within an hour."[29]

"We'll kill everyone," was the response. "That means the hostages and we'll die ourselves."[30]

Exactly five days after prisoners took control of Attica, the prison was retaken with a fury that dwarfed the violence of the initial uprising.

Army helicopters made about ten passes over the prison walls dropping canisters of teargas before a police helicopter flew over announcing, "Surrender peacefully. You will not be hurt. Do not harm the hostages. You will not be harmed. Sit or lay down. Place your hands on top of your heads."[31]

As soon as the teargas was being dropped, D-Yard was showered in a hail of police bullets and a thousand state troopers stormed the prison. From outside a blanket of teargas billowed over the thirty-foot prison walls.

"You murdering bastards!" shouted Attorney and observers' committee member William Kunstler at the sound of gunfire. "They're shooting them! They're murdering them!"[32]

"It looks like war," a prison official said as he emerged from the cloud of teargas.[33]

Twenty-eight prisoners and nine hostages were reported dead after ninety minutes of police gunfire. There were at least forty others rushed away on stretchers. Authorities code-named the assault "Operation Go."

"The troopers were starting to come out into the yard,"

a state trooper recalled, "and when some of the niggers attacked them, we had to shoot them. I could see a whole load of troopers come out, probably 25 or 30 together, and they came out slowly and they told the prisoners to kneel down in front of them to surrender. Then we covered them. If any one of them stood up to attack, we shot him... I shot but I don't know if I hit anybody. Everyone was shooting; everyone was falling for a few seconds... We yelled to the prisoners 'Face down! Don't move, nigger! You're dead!'... The bad ones we made crawl."[34]

Afterwards, ranking police told their men, "Everything went beautiful."[35]

Oswald announced to a sea of reporters, "It became apparent to me that further delay would jeopardize the lives of the hostages and would threaten the prison system of the state."[36]

Rebelling prisoners, who were known not to have any guns, were all reported to have died from bullet wounds. The nine dead hostages were called "homicides."

A public relations officer for the State Corrections Department announced that the dead hostages were all found with their throats slashed, and that some were castrated.

"Different weapons were used to kill the hostages," he said. "There was no indication that the prisoners had guns."[37]

Representatives from Governor Rockefeller's office said that a number of the hostages had been dead for several hours before the prison was retaken.

The bodies were taken to a makeshift morgue set up in the prison's maintenance building.

Reports from area hospitals immediately conflicted with official statements. A hostage who died in one hospital was reported to have a fatal gunshot wound. Another hostage who survived was also reported to have suffered a gunshot wound to the hip. A third hostage in a separate hospital had a gunshot wound to the head.[38] A fourth surviving hostage was hospitalized with bullet wounds in the leg, chest and neck.[39]

Governor Rockefeller blamed the deaths on "highly organized, revolutionary tactics of militants." He said the prisoners "rejected all efforts at a peaceful settlement, forced a confrontation and carried out cold-blooded killings they had threatened from the onset… We can be grateful that the skill and courage of the state police and correction officers, supported by the National Guard and sheriff's deputies, saved the lives of 32 hostages and that their restraint held down casualties among prisoners as well." [40]

Outside of the Governor's office protests raged. Crowds of angry citizens came together under banners that read, "Governor Pig, You Are Wanted For Murder" and "Mass Murderer Of Attica." [41]

William Kunstler charged, "This will go down in history as a bloody mistake. They sold the lives far too cheaply. I guess they always do." [42]

"They are guilty of murder," accused Bobby Seale. "The best thing to do would be to charge Oswald and the others with first-degree, outright mass murder." [43]

"After San Quentin [the media] showed the funeral of George Jackson. Who cares about that?" a wife of a freed hostage disagreed. "They're in Attica because they broke society's rules. It's their own fault and they have a debt to pay… I don't know why outfits like the Black Panthers think they can tell everybody how to run the world. It's just outrageous."

On Main Street in the village of Attica, reporters found a couple of teenagers talking.

"How's your father?" asked the girl.

"He's okay," a boy replied. "The guy who was supposed to kill him had his arm shot off."

The village of Attica was all but consumed by the week's events. The 2,875 citizens barely outnumbered the population in their prison, and half of the village's workforce was employed there. The Mayor of Attica had a second job as a correctional officer. Since the riot broke out you couldn't come or go from the village without passing through checkpoints set up by the local and state police.

"This town has never seen such an accumulation of police power," a county sheriff's deputy pronounced. [44]

Tensions were high among the townsfolk of Attica. A county sheriff's deputy, who coined the village of Attica "honor America country," spoke of complaints about "the coloreds" from locals anxious to see the hostages released and their small-town lives back to normal.

"I've never felt endangered here," said a woman who lived across the street from the prison, "although a few years ago, I would have said this could never happen."[45]

"You have Harlem and the South Bronx and Bed-Stuy inside the walls," a *Times* editorial spelled out, "and they're being guarded by farmers who are scared as hell of them."[46]

A seventeen year-old, who used to tell people who weren't familiar with Attica that he lived between Buffalo and Rochester, was shocked at the changes taking place in his hometown, "I never thought I'd live to see the day when Attica became a national issue."[47]

Until September of 1971, Attica was best known for it's nine churches, two banks, two lumber mills, the Attica Garden Club, the Attica Rod and Gun Club, a crate and box factory, their historical society, grange and annual rodeo show. It would never be the same.

Commissioner Oswald wasted no time before reading his public justification for the more than forty lives lost in the hasty assault to the mob of hungry reporters gathered in front of the prison walls.

"Armed rebellion of the type we have faced threatens the destruction of our free society. We cannot permit that destruction to happen."

He said the actions of the Attica Brothers were, "not different from their behavior on the street, where several were convicted of serious assaults, manslaughter and murder."[48]

Front-page articles across the country on September 14, 1971, told a much different story.

After official autopsies were performed, medical examiners exposed what was obvious by just looking at the hostages' corpses, "All died of gunshot wounds. There were no cut throats, no mutilations or castrations."[49]

Some of the hostages' bodies had as many as twelve gunshot wounds.

Even Commissioner Oswald reluctantly admitted that the

hostages were killed by police gunfire during Monday's retaking of the prison.

Assistant Commissioner Walter Dunbar applauded the assault regardless, "When you think about the number involved and when you say it only resulted in about 38 dead... I'd say it was remarkable."[50]

A grandmother of a prisoner who only had a week to go when he was killed in the assault was so upset she told reporters if she had a machine gun she would cut Governor Rockefeller down.[51]

"There was no slashing," a relative of killed hostage Carl Valone said after personally viewing the body. "He was not even touched... We feel that Carl was killed not by the prisoners but by a bullet that had the name Rockefeller written on it."[52]

Sam noticed someone new in the yard eyeing the chess games, and introduced himself.

"Hey brother, how ya doing?"

"I'm alright, how are you?" the stranger answered, nervous and defensive as he should've been his first days in a new prison.

"My name is Sam."

John Boncore was an American Indian living on the wintry streets of Buffalo. He tried to rob a corner store, pretending his finger was the barrel of a pistol in his coat pocket. His ploy failed and he slipped on the icy stairs fleeing the scene. Nothing was stolen and there was no weapon. He was sentenced to eight years for Attempted Robbery. John found himself in Attica just weeks before the rebellion.

"You play chess?" Sam asked.

They grew close quickly. They were the only ones in the yard who could give each other a good game.

"You know," Sam got to talking with John one day in the yard, "I never really knew too many Native brothers, but you've got a really proud history and are valiant fighters."

Sam told John that most prisoners were locked up because they couldn't sustain a decent living, that they were victims of vicious economic systems, and were being exploited by the government and a capitalist system that was based on profit and private property.

"He was really talking about the necessity of armed revolution in America, to overthrow the capitalist structure," John remembers. "I automatically was just cueing right into what he was saying. He was giving me definition to a lot of anger I had… He was my initial mentor."

"Somehow he had documents printed up and he would teach people about revolutionary figures. One of the things that Sam turned me on to was the writings of George Jackson."

Sam worked as a freelance organizer in Attica, slipping prisoners copies of *The Iced Pig* and trying to unite the brothers across the barriers between races, cellblocks and organizations.

Sam and John kept rapping and playing chess each day in the yard, they even got a couple of games in during the uprising.

LIKE A REAL REVOLUTIONARY

John vividly remembers the moment when the prisoners broke loose.

"We came to a stop and there was maybe about eight guards there. Then there was this tall, black brother, who was a known Panther, he said to the captain, 'Why'd you lock them brothers up last night?' The captain said, 'I don't know fellas, but we'll look into it.' Then the brother said, 'You're fucking full of shit honkey!' and he punched him right in the mouth and knocked him down."

"That's when Sam came out from somewhere and kicked him in the side of the ribs. And that's when I turned around and yelled 'Take this motherfucking place now!' and it was just like a spark and a prairie fire."

The few dozen prisoners in the corridor with Sam and John, including Richard X Clark, L. D. Barclay and Tommy Hicks, overpowered the guards and ripped down a gate separating them from their brothers in other blocks. Within minutes prisoners had control of most of the prison.[1]

Rumors spread about the high-profile political prisoner in the heart of the most significant prison uprising in American history. "Sam Melville... rigged booby traps to keep the police at bay."[2] "Samuel Melville... was probably stockpiling Molotov cocktails."[3]

Sam may not have been the most visible prisoner during the uprising, but everyone knew they'd be looking for him when they came over the walls. "You know the beef I'm up for?" Sam said to a brother before the prison was retaken, "If those troopers come over the wall I'm dead."[4]

Commissioner Oswald considered Sam one of the seven leaders of the rebellion, claiming Sam "had the reputation of being one of the most violent revolutionaries in the whole country."[5] He claimed Sam led the group that stormed the prison's metal shop, taking hostages and using the machinery to make weapons for the rebelling prisoners.

"Sam Melville was the rebel field commander," Oswald wrote, "the man who ordered the forging of hundreds of weapons, the construction of barricades and trenches and the refining of explosives from paint thinner, fertilizer and fire extinguisher compounds. He was even manufacturing what appeared to be an amateur rocket-launcher for use against low-flying helicopters."[6]

"These barricades consisted of steel and metal tables, benches, partitions, link fencing wired to railings, the lot festooned with metal prongs on which the troopers might be impaled. The link fencing and other elements of the barricades could be electrified – as we had been warned they would be. Near each of these barricades were Molotov cocktails and fifty gallon drums filled with inflammable liquids. Mattresses were being soaked with these fluids, presumably to be ignited if and when we launched an attack. There was a long, shallow slit trench, dug during the rebellion, protecting D-Yard from any attack launched from the corridor tunnels."

Oswald continued, "There was an additional barricade, an individual barricade, for the urban guerrilla who had put this whole thing together. On ground level, behind Times Square, out of line of fire from any of the surrounding roofs, was a steel and metal barricade for Sam Melville... This was an admirably central position, right up to the front line, but there could be no escape from a position that far forward. Sam Melville obviously meant to win or die."[7]

Sam was the first Attica Brother that William Kunstler formally met when he joined the observers' committee.

"I'm Sam Melville, and I'd like to say hello to you. We have many mutual friends."

Kunstler heard that Sam was the one who nominated Herbert X. Blyden to the negotiating committee, calling him forward through the bullhorn over the crowd of Attica Brothers just after they gained control of the prison.

"Our lives are at stake," Sam pepped Brother Herb, "and it's vital that we get the blocks together."

Sam knew Herb from doing time at The Tombs and worked closely with him on the manifesto drafts of the Attica Liberation Faction in the weeks before the uprising. They also organized the vigil for George Jackson and got numerous prisoners to sign a sympathy letter to Jackson's mother.

116

"Without Sam's signature," Herb said, "the letter to Mrs. Jackson just wouldn't have meant as much."

Brother Herb was unanimously voted in as the Chairman of the negotiating committee. Sam didn't have direct involvement in the drawn out negotiations but stayed close, offering suggestions and providing security.

The last Kunstler saw of Sam his arms were linked in a line of Attica Brothers who were protecting the negotiations from the main body of prisoners. Kunstler told Sam he'd see him later.

"I hope so," Sam replied without breaking his hold in the human chain. "But whatever happens, tell everyone that people here are as together as I once hoped they could be on the outside."[8]

Name:
     Samuel Melville

Cause and Date of Death:
     Exsanguination from wound to the shoulder and damage to the left lung. 9/13/71

Location where Died:
     D Yard

Weapon:
     Shotgun

Origin of Gunfire:
     D Catwalk[9]

"Mad Bomber Melville was killed by a sharpshooter as he was running with four homemade bombs ready to blow up a 500-gallon fuel tank," reported the *New York Times* the day after police retook the prison.[10]

"Samuel J. Melville, who was given the nickname 'Mad Bomber' and was convicted of blasting eight buildings, was among the prisoners killed in the Attica Correctional Facility assault," the *Buffalo Evening News* reported. "Melville, 35, was cut down in the prison yard by a state police sharpshooter."[11]

"Samuel J. Melville," another article read, "the terrorist radical who pleaded guilty to the 1969 bombings of eight buildings in Manhattan, was one of the Attica prisoners killed Monday."[12]

Yet another newspaper depicted Sam "dying like a real revolutionary, firebomb in one hand, spear in another, leaping at a shotgun-firing State Trooper."[13]

The papers all reported Sam's death long before the names of any other inmates were released to the public. In fact, the prison officials' version of Sam's death was announced to the media right after the assault, as an example to justify the deadly force used in retaking the prison.

A former F.B.I. agent, who was given a $200 award from F.B.I. Director J. Edgar Hoover for his part in busting Sam, Jane and Dave, shared his thoughts on Sam's death, "Fortunately for the people of New York City, Sam Melville was killed during the Attica Prison riots in 1971, with bombs strapped to his body."[14]

Another account has Sam dying in the arms of Robin Palmer after being shot. Palmer was close with Sam on the streets before Sam was arrested. They were reunited in Attica after he followed in Sam's footsteps and was convicted of a firebombing aimed against the Vietnam War.[15]

Richard X Clark was one of a number of Attica Brothers whose personal accounts contradicted the media reports, suggesting that Sam lived through the assault only to be singled out for execution after the prison was retaken. Brother Richard wrote of seeing Sam just after the five to ten minute barrage of gunfire had stopped. Sam was wrapped in a blanket and had tears in his eyes when he looked at Brother Richard and said, "We still did our thing."[16]

A year later, The Official Report of the New York State Special Commission on Attica ruled that accounts of Sam being executed were unsubstantiated. The Commission made public an official account of the details of Sam's murder.

Samuel Melville was killed at least five

minutes after the assault began by one rifled slug from a state police shotgun fired by a B.C.I. [Bureau of Criminal Investigation, better known as the "subversive squad"] investigator standing atop Times Square...

The officer testified that he saw an inmate in D Yard bobbing up and down behind a crudely fashioned bunker made of fertilizer bags against the wall of D Catwalk. The B.C.I. agent said he lifted his gasmask and yelled to the inmate to stop his activity behind the bunker. The inmate appeared, he said, with what appeared to be a Molotov cocktail in his right hand. Fearing he would throw the Molotov cocktail, the investigator said he fired one shot from the shotgun, striking the inmate in the chest.

Another member of the B.C.I. from the same unit who was standing next to him corroborated his account. However, neither man was absolutely certain that the inmate was about to throw a Molotov cocktail, and neither could say whether it was lit. The investigator who did not fire said that 15 minutes later he went down to D Yard to examine the body and could not find a Molotov cocktail near it, although there was a bucket of such devices in the bunker...

It is, however, questioned that Melville was not shot accidentally or during the initial wave of shooting from the roofs or the catwalks. He was shot by a law enforcement officer who admitted aiming at him and stated his belief that he was justified in shooting him. [17]

"I saw troopers coming down the ladders from the tunnels and Times Square and start to move towards the hostages," an Attica Brother recalled a much different story than the Commission. "'They're here already,' I said to Sam. Sam turned to me. 'Well,' he said, 'we did the best we could.' We shook hands and I understood that we would go out and surrender. Then I heard a shot. I turned to Sam and saw that he had been shot by a bullet in the chest."[18]

Another Attica Brother remembers a man who he thought was Sam trying to surrender, "He had his hands folded on top of his head as the loudspeaker in the helicopter said to. He was walking towards the wall. A trooper was standing on the wall. The guy kept walking towards him and a trooper shot him in the chest.[19]

John Boncore also remembers when police retook the prison. As troopers were pointing their guns at Boncore and beating him with their rifle butts, he heard yelling, "Melville, you're dead meat!"

He looked up in the chaos and got a glimpse of someone he thought was Sam, gripping his chest and falling to the ground.

"It's like they got justice there. They got revenge is what they got."

"He was a great dude, man, he was just a hell of a great dude. We always said he died like a warrior. He died for what he believed in."[20]

"Certain people were murdered in cold blood, were taken out because of who they were," recalled Liz Fink, lead council of the Attica Brothers' legal team. "Certainly there's no question in our mind, and has never been a question in our mind, that Sam was one of two, or three, or four people... certainly Tommy Hicks... that was definitely executed.

"Sam tried to keep a very low profile, but if you look at some of the footage that comes out of the rebellion... you see that he's sitting right in the back of everything. And you know he was a major player in what was happening and what was going down... He and Tommy Hicks, were... shall we say, the ideological backbone of what was happening."

"He was in this company called Five Company, which was what was called the Grading Company, but really it was the company where all the trouble makers were... [the prison authorities] put Sam in the Grading Company because he was extremely militant and he was out there trying to organize everybody… Many of the people who died in the assault were in Five Company, and many of them were shot and killed in cold blood because of who they were. Tommy Hicks locked next to Sam… He was an unbelievably militant person and him and Sam hooked up and they were the ideological basis of what was happening. If you look at the negotiating table, there's a group of inmates in the back who are sort of not participating but clearly right in the middle of what's happening, and one of those people is Sam Melville."

"It was a slaughter because they wanted it to be a slaughter. They planned that. That was what was gonna happen. They were gonna show people what happens when you took this kind of step. There just wasn't any question about it. None if it was necessary. It all could have been put down without a shot… They didn't want that. They wanted maximum destruction, maximum murder… They were gonna kill 'em, and they did. It's as simple as that. Murder them in cold blood."[21]

"He was good. He was one of the sweetest, nicest, people… He was a mass of contradictions," friend and fellow revolutionary Sharon Berman remembered Sam back on the streets of the East Village. "He was a very simplistic individual. He had no sense that what he was doing could be wrong, once he made up his mind. He felt that what he was doing, he was doing for the betterment of humanity, and if he didn't believe that, he couldn't have done anything… You lose your best people in those kinds of activities, the people who could make a difference."

Sharon visited Sam a number of times when he was locked at the West Street holding facility. That was before she found herself behind bars.

Sharon, two other women and four men, including Robin Palmer, were arrested firebombing Citibank on East 91st Street and Madison Avenue in Manhattan, in an effort against the Bank's involvement in the Vietnam War. They were set up. One of the men was an informant.

Sharon was serving a four-year sentence when she heard news of the Attica uprising.

"I was sitting in the recreation room, and all of us were glued to the T.V. And it was known that I had a relationship with [Robin Palmer]. What the warden was doing was, everyone who had a boyfriend or a husband at Attica, she was calling in to tell them how their partner was doing, if they had lived or died. She called me in to tell me about [Robin Palmer], that he was fine. I really wanted to ask about Sam, but I didn't have the nerve, and he wasn't my man so I couldn't really ask them for that. So I went back to the rec. room… The [television] announcer said, 'You'll be happy to know that the Mad Bomber was killed when the state retook Attica'… I couldn't really show how mournful I was that Sam was gone. Then a few weeks latter this rabbi came to visit me that I had never met before. He was one of the traveling chaplains. He had met Sam at Attica, and him and I just sort of sat together in the visiting room, and cried."[22]

"I have my own suspicions that Sam was gunned down because he was an apostate," William Kunstler wrote, "a white man who had managed to leap racial barriers."[23]

Kunstler spoke of Sam in his final speech before a graduating class in Sam's hometown of Buffalo. Kunstler recalled a conversation they had in D-Yard the day before police retook the prison.

"Sam, where'd you get that name Melville?"

"I took it," Sam told him. "My real name is not Melville, but I was so impressed by what [Herman Melville] was saying in Moby Dick that I took that name."

"So?," Kunstler pressed, "What about Moby Dick? It's just a whale story."

"No, It's not, Bill," Sam explained. "The white whale is evil, that swims on… unconquerable. Everybody dies on the Pequod. The Pequod is smashed to smithereens by the whale. Ahab is lashed by the harpoon lanyard to the whale's back and is drowned, the men in the long boat are destroyed, but one man goes back to sea."[24]

Shortly after 7:30 p.m. on September 17, 1971, four days after Sam was killed, an explosion ripped apart Commissioner

LIKE A REAL REVOLUTIONARY

Oswald's new office in the State Department of Corrections.

An Albany Police Chief said the bomb erupted from an air conditioning and heating duct in a restroom in the front part of the building's ninth floor.

A warning call was made moments before the explosion. The caller identified herself as a member of the Weather Underground.

Newspapers reported text of the communiqué.

> Tonight we attacked the head offices of the New York State Department of Correction in Albany. Tomorrow thousands of people will demonstrate in New York and around the country against this racist slaughter. We must continue to make the Rockefellers, the Oswalds, the Reagans and the Nixons pay for their crimes.[25]
>
> We only wish we could do more to show the courageous prisoners at Attica, San Quentin and other 20th century slave ships that they are not alone in their fight for the right to live.[26]

EPILOGUE

Sam's body was flown to Washington Square Church, on West Fourth Street in Manhattan, for a three-day wake so people from the movement could pay their last respects.

Jane Alpert even managed to sneak in for a tearful goodbye.

Thanks to arrangements made by some of her supporters working as lookouts, setting up safe houses, and providing transportation, Jane dressed in a disguise and had a private 2 a.m. visit before slipping back out of sight.[1]

Ten days after Jane first went underground, her bail was revoked, a warrant was put out for her arrest, and Dave Hughey was brought into court.

"In my opinion," the judge said, "I don't think Mr. Hughey will be here at the date of the sentence."

Dave's bail was revoked and he was immediately taken into custody.[2]

Jane jumped bail intending to join an "intense, life risking," underground struggle. She expected a full-blown revolution to topple America within six months, and aimed to break Sam out of prison before it went down. She claimed to have been making plans for Sam's prison break with the Weathermen before she lost contact with them.[3]

After Sam was killed, Jane wrote a 40-page "Profile of Sam Melville," her first public account of the events leading up to the Manhattan bombings. She sent the manuscript to her lawyer and it was published along with a number of Sam's prison letters in a book titled, Letters From Attica that listed its author as the post-mortem "Samuel Melville." In failed efforts to hunt Jane down, the F.B.I. questioned the publisher and subpoenaed Jane's lawyer to a grand jury.[4]

"Melville's death brought Alpert high celebrity in radical circles as a sort of gold star widow of the left," Time magazine wrote.[5]

But life underground turned out to be "a rather unadventurous and secluded existence" for Jane,[6] and "psychologically difficult." Her lawyer explained that Jane lived a "respectable" life as a fugitive, not engaging in guerrilla, or

EPILOGUE

even illegal activity, and holding a series of mundane jobs for about four and a half years. [7] She eventually did find members of the Weather Underground but the meetings only left her feeling increasingly alienated. Jane claimed it was her experiences underground that changed her mind about revolution. She said she discovered a "bedrock conservatism" while running around the country as a fugitive, deciding that her past political views were "not particularly relevant to what's going on today" and "basically destructive to women."

"As I traveled," she said, "I slowly became aware that nothing was less relevant to the lives of most people in this country."[8]

"It was like a primal scream rising up in me," Jane recalled, "I realized I had never been what I seemed to be then... [Sam] was on his own sacrificial course – and it had done great destruction to me."[9]

In May of 1973, Jane published an article titled "MOTHER RIGHT: A New Feminist Theory," making public her conversion from a "serious militant leftist" to a "radical feminist." She sent the article to *Ms. Magazine* and other feminist periodicals, along with a note and a copy of her fingerprints as proof of authenticity.

The first half of "MOTHER RIGHT" was an open letter from Jane to the Weather Underground, criticizing the organization and the entire left, for sexist practices. The open letter claimed to be a minor breach of the Weather Underground's security by exposing private correspondence Jane was having with fugitive members of the organization.

In it, Jane made her first public accusations of Sam's "male supremacy." She claimed, "I was very much pressured, against my own sense of tactics and timing, into playing the role I did in the group of radical bombers Melville half-led, half-dragged along with him."

The open letter ended with a bold and highly criticized statement about the Attica dead. Pounding home her political conversion Jane wrote, "I will mourn the loss of 42 male supremacists no longer."[10]

Finally, in November of 1974, Jane made arrangements with her lawyer to turn herself in, agreeing to full cooperation with the F.B.I.[11]

"This is really the happiest day of my life,"[12] Jane said to reporters, "All I have to say is that this is a great relief. It's an important step in my life and I feel more at home with myself and my family... It was the right thing to do."[13]

"I'm not that person anymore," Jane told the *New York Times*, "I have tried for five years to understand as well as I could the craziness that came over me... I am now horrified to think what I have to take responsibility for."[14]

In court, Jane's lawyer pleaded, "The girl who stood before Your Honor four and a half years ago is not the same woman who stands before you now... She is no longer in the grip of the mistaken ideology which caused her to flee; the war is over and the man with whom she was in love and for whom she pleaded guilty is now dead," he argued. "She did it all for Melville – even pleaded guilty for him."[15]

Jane added, "I realized well over a year ago that I had been completely wrong in jumping bail... My goal is to stop living the life I've been living."[16]

To help reach that goal Jane was interviewed on national television by Ann Medina of *ABC News*, who introduced the feminist as "Sam Melville's lover, his follower."

In it, Jane explained that the reason that people who were opposed to the Vietnam War turned to urban guerrilla warfare, was that they "did feel passionately about the war [but] failed to find outlets in demonstrations, or petitioning, or any of the things that had been traditionally available to us as citizens."

But when Jane was asked if it still made sense to her now, she hesitatingly responded, "It... I don't think it's too strong to say that it horrifies me."

Jane told the national television audience that her life underground "was like being in prison because nobody else knew who I was and I lived in a kind of isolated cell of my own existence and... in psychological ways I had to very much find my own way."

She took the opportunity to make a public apology, "I do

feel sorry for what happened and I've spent, really the last year, reliving a lot of that detail and coming to grips with it, and I'm sorry to have ever acted to endanger human lives. I don't think that's a particularly forgivable thing."[17]

Jane faced a maximum of ten years in prison and a $10,000 fine for conspiracy and bail jumping. The case was seen by the same judge who handled the bombing conspiracy five years earlier. This time, however, she received over thirty months less for the bombing conspiracy than the four-to-six years she was originally sentenced to in 1970, and only nine months for jumping bail. Her total time served was a year and eight months, with seven months taken off her sentence for her good behavior as a prisoner. Dave Hughey, who didn't jump bail but also didn't cooperate with investigators, did a total of two and a half years behind bars.[18]

Authorities and reporters all wanted to know what other radical fugitives Jane knew from the underground and who would be surfacing next. It seemed that Jane had little information to offer until Pat Swinton was suddenly arrested just three months later.

"Since she surrendered last November," the news reported, "Jane Alpert has been strongly attacked by militant feminists who believe she informed on Pat Swinton and other fugitives and fear that she will testify against Miss Swinton before a grand jury."[19]

An issue of *Midnight Special*, a prisoner's newsletter sent out to 4,000 prisoners across the country, labeled Jane an informant, naming the women's prison where she was being held, and stating, "We feel it is necessary for us to print this in order to point out to the sisters inside that there is a traitor in their midst."

"I have heard that the direct lead on some of these apprehended people came from another radical," Jane's attorney admitted but insisted that Jane didn't turn anyone in. "These reports that she is the informer who led to recent arrests of radical fugitives are completely false. It is outrageous. Singling out an inmate like that is totally irresponsible. People have been beaten up in prison because of something like that… She's in a terrible crunch."

At Pat's trial, Jane gave what reporters called "a vehement renunciation of her radical past… an emotional denunciation," where she called the bombings "terrible mistakes."

Yet Jane surprisingly joined Dave Hughey and refused to testify against Pat. The judge gave them each an additional four months behind bars for contempt of court.

"Miss Alpert said she had been repeatedly abused, harassed and threatened by other prisoners while serving her previous sentence," an article reported. "She stressed that her refusal to testify in the Swinton trial was based on her fear of being killed in retaliation by prisoners or radicals."[20]

Attorney Liz Fink recalls representing former political prisoner Susan Saxe after Saxe had a run-in with Jane in New York's Metropolitan Correctional Center, "Susan... was waiting in reception... and the Warden's Secretary came in... she took one look at Susan and she ran out, and that person was Jane Alpert."

To save money, inmates fill a number of jobs needed to run the prisons. Secretary for the Warden is a prisoner job that requires a considerable amount of trust and loyalty, and puts the prisoner in a position of power through their relationship with the Warden. Of all the prisoners at the Metropolitan Correctional Center, the Warden's Secretary was Jane Alpert.

"Two hours later, I mean *two hours*, Susan was transferred to Nassau County Jail, where she was treated abysmally," Fink explained. "Susan had no relationship to Jane at all, it was just that Jane took one look at her and said 'Oh No!'... 'I don't want to be near this person, I'm worried for my safety.' It was a bunch of horseshit, and it really was dreadful for Susan... It was a very hard and difficult situation and it was all caused by Jane's paranoia at seeing Susan."[21]

"I consider Jane responsible for my arrest," Pat Swinton said the night before her trial began, "but I never thought and still don't think that Jane would ever intentionally turn someone in to the authorities. Her mistakes were ones of bad judgment. But they were bad mistakes."

Pat was acquitted of all charges relating to the Manhattan bombings because the prosecution's key witness was George Demmerle, who knew so little of her that he couldn't even identify her. When Dave and Jane refused to testify against Pat the government essentially had no case against her.

"The government's case was discredited," Pat said, "because it hinged on either trying to jam people who were obviously not willing to be there as witnesses against me, or on using the testimony of informers – and informers repel everybody."[22]

The Weather Underground continued much in the same fashion as Sam and his accomplices, bombing over twenty buildings across the United States including dynamite blasts that damaged the State Department, the U.S. Capitol and the Pentagon. They bombed a U.S. Army base in San Francisco to celebrate the Cuban Revolution exactly one year after Sam's bombing of the United Fruit Company for the same purpose. The Weather Underground was much better educated, funded and organized than Sam and his group, and have gained much wider publicity. Their attacks continued until members began to surface in the late-seventies and early-eighties, mostly facing relatively minor criminal charges.

In 1981, after the statute of limitations for the Manhattan bombings was up, Jane published a personal memoir that told a significantly different version of the story than she wrote in her "Profile of Sam Melville." Her memoir made numerous damning allegations and a sweeping psychoanalysis that pointed ultimate blame and responsibility for the bombings, and a number of her personal issues, on the insanity, manipulation and sexism of Sam and others in the movement.

The *New York Times* reviewed the book saying, "To ascribe all the convulsive changes of those brief months to her obsessive love for Sam Melville is, judging by either the political rhetoric of the time or contemporary standards of feminist self-respect, a stunningly revisionist posture... The narrative lends disturbing new meaning to the phrase 'sexual politics,' and the absence of analysis will be especially distressing to those who once saw Miss Alpert as the model of an intellectual revolutionary."[23]

Jane's book was highly criticized for revisionist politics

but also made a number of valid points about sexism and other forms of stupidity within the revolutionary struggle, and it told a story that I found interesting enough to eventually begin the research that would lead to this book.

It is not my intention to prove or disprove Jane's allegations. Debates have been raging for a long time between people who were actually involved in those specific situations. I encourage interested readers to do their own research and education on issues of oppression within liberation struggles. None of us are near perfection and we could all use some help when it comes to walking our talk.

Jane's political conversion, and especially her unknown level of cooperation with federal law enforcement agencies, made her writings highly questionable as sources. Something Jane wrote while underground, for example, might directly conflict with something she wrote after she decided to face legal consequences and cooperate with the F.B.I. Of course other sources are questionable too, including a macho and heavily biased memoir written by the former Chief of Detectives for the N.Y.P.D., and a number of newspaper articles of very poor journalistic quality. In all cases I've attempted to use my best judgment when citing the limited supply of sources I had available for this book.

The personal interviews I was able to secure were invaluable, and here I'd like to thank John "Splitting The Sky" Boncore, Ray Luc Levasseur, William Crain, Sharon Berman and Liz Fink for their cooperation and encouragement.

I also greatly appreciate the assistance of Karen Campbell, Ellie Epp, James Sparrell, Tomas Kalmar, Ralph Lutts, Shelley Vermilya, Chris Hables Gray and Robert Buchanan of Goddard College, as well as Luce Guillén-Givins and Theresa Baker for their invaluable proofreading and editing assistance, David Gilbert for his commentary and guidance, and the Vanderbilt Television News Archive, the Attica Historical Society, the Buffalo and Erie County Public Library, and Arissa Media Group.

The simplistic political analysis in this book is not nearly enough. I encourage every reader to analyze the issues raised in this book in relation to the circumstances in your own lives, and to act on those understandings. The standard theories and strategies used to achieve liberation in America today aren't exactly liberating us. Do not let the dogmatic standards of a failing liberation struggle dictate how you think or act.

I didn't write this to idealize Sam Melville as a hero. He suffered from real life issues like the rest of us. He went through an intense personal struggle with drugs. He made considerable mistakes handling relationships with the people he loved, including his child. Much has been written about the sexism of radical men in the 1960s, and Sam is certainly subject to that constructive criticism.

I wrote this because I believe the lessons that this piece of history has to offer are essential to our progress. As a movement, we need to learn from past mistakes and successes. We won't be able to learn those lessons if we continue to let history be written and unwritten by the kind of people who want us to think Sam Melville was a "Mad Bomber."

I know there are a number of us who can take inspiration from someone who was far from perfect but never gave up the struggle. Someone who came to a revolutionary perspective from a personal experience of poverty and hard work, and who moved on this understanding by uniting with people from other races and walks of life against a common oppression. Someone who made the ultimate sacrifice for what they believed in.

I included all of the apparently contradicting accounts of Sam's death with equal weight in the last chapter because I believe there is some truth to all of them and they all need to be heard to get the best possible understanding of the full truth. It is both history and martyr mythology, which is no different than any of the other information we constantly digest. I don't expect to ever know the exact details of Sam's last moments on Earth, but I believe I know how he died, because I know how he lived.

If a movement as "together" as what Sam came to know in his last few days on Earth existed outside Attica's walls, a revolution might have been won many years ago. And maybe today Sam would have been making up for his failures as a father, a comrade and a lover, and singing in the opera.

NOTES

CHAPTER 1

1. <u>A Town Designed For Better Living</u> <http://www.tonawanda.ny.us/htm/more_about.htm>.

2. Jane Alpert, <u>Growing Up Underground</u> (New York: William Morrow & Company, Inc., 1981) 119.

3. Carl J. Pelleck, "Nightmare Ended His Dream: Bomber Melville Among the Attica Dead" <u>New York Post</u> 14 September 1971: 2.

4. Alpert, <u>Growing</u> 120.

5. Jane Alpert, "Profile of Sam Melville" <u>Letters From Attica</u> by Samuel Melville (New York: William Morrow & Company, Inc., 1972) 14-15.

6. Alpert, "Profile" 16.

7. Alpert, <u>Growing</u> 112.

8. Alpert, <u>Growing</u> 140-141.

9. Alpert, <u>Growing</u> 195-196.

10. Liz Fink, personal interview with author, 16 January 2007.

11. Albert A. Seedman and Peter Hellman, <u>Chief!</u> (New York: Arthur Fields Books, Inc., 1974) 226.

12. "George Metesky: New York City's Mad Bomber" <u>Court TV Crime Library: Criminal Minds and Methods</u> <http://www.crimelibrary.com/terrorists_spies/terrorists/metesky/2.html>.

13. Pierre Vallieres, <u>White Niggers of America</u> (New York: Monthly Review Press, 1971) 282-288.

14. Mitch Abidor, "Le Front de Libération du Québec" <u>Canada History Archive</u> <<u>www.marxists.org/history/canada/quebec/F.L.Q./</u> <u>introduction.htm</u>>. "Front de Libération du Québec" <u>Answers.Com</u> <<u>www.answers.com/topic/front-de-lib-ration-du-qu-bec</u>>.

15. Alpert, <u>Growing</u> 155.

16. Jane Alpert, <u>RAT Subterranean News</u> 12-18 June, 1969: 4.

17. Alpert, <u>Growing</u> 170.

CHAPTER 2

1. Jane Alpert, Growing Up Underground (New York: William Morrow & Company,
1981) 188.
2. Albert A. Seedman and Peter Hellman, Chief! (New York: Arthur Fields Books, Inc., 1974) 214-216.
3. Seedman, 215.
4. Alpert, Growing 192.
5. Seedman, 122-123.
6. Alpert, Growing 187-200.
7. Liberation News Service, "United Fruit Pier Bombed" Rat Subterranean News 12-26 August, 1969: 6.
8. Alpert, Growing 199-202.
9. J.Q. Rat, "All the Low Down on the Blow Down" Rat Subterranean News, 12-25 November 1969: 3.
10. Alpert, Growing 199-202
11. Seedman 210-211.
12. "Munitions Plant in Jersey Ruined by Blast: None Hurt" New York Times 13 July, 1969: 56.
13. Alpert, Growing 200-205.
14. Alpert, Growing 206.
15. Lawrence Van Gelder, "Blast Rips Bank in Financial Area" New York Times 21 August 1969: 47.
16. Van Gelder.
17. Cy Egan and Steven Marcus, "Hunt Bomber in Bank Blast" New York Post 21 August 1969: 1.
18. Van Gelder.
19. Seedman, 212.
20. Seedman, 214.
21. Alpert, Growing 206-208.
22. Rat.
23. "Wall St. Bombing" Rat Subterranean News 27 August – 9 September 1969: 3.
24. Jane Alpert, "Profile of Sam Melville" Letters From Attica by Samuel Melville (New York: William Morrow & Company, Inc., 1972) 29-30.
25. Alpert, Growing 210-211.
26. "Wall St. Bombing."

NOTES

27. Alpert, Growing 211.

CHAPTER 3

1. Jane Alpert, Growing Up Underground (New York: William Morrow & Company, 1981) 208-209.
2. "Rebels Blast Fed Plaza" Rat Subterranean News 8-21 October 1969: 4.
3. Thomas A. Johnson, "Explosion Wrecks U.S. Offices Here" New York Times 20 September 1969: 46.
4. Johnson.
5. Sandor M. Polster, "Blast Rips Federal Bldg. Here" New York Post 9 September 1969: 1.
6. Alpert, Growing.
Jane Alpert, "Profile of Sam Melville" Letters From Attica by Samuel Melville (New York: William Morrow & Company, Inc., 1972).
7. Alpert, Growing 212-214.
8. Alpert, Growing 214.
9. Alpert, Growing 214-215.
10. Seedman, 218-220.
11. Seedman, 221-222.
12. Alpert, Growing 217-218.
13. Seedman, 214.
14. Seedman, 220.
15. Alpert, Growing 217.
16. Seedman, 222.
17. Alpert, Growing 218.
18. "Draft Center Here Damaged by Blast" New York Times 8 October 1969: 1.
19. Alpert, Growing 219.
20. A Daughter of the American Revolution, "It's Just a Shot Away" RAT Subterranean News, 17 April 1970: 4.
21. "Bang? Boom!" RAT Subterranean News 29 October – 12 November 1969: 10.
22. "Draft Center Here Damaged by Blast."
23. "Draft Center Here Damaged by Blast."
24. Ron Dobbin and Nancy Seely, "Induction HQ Is Shut Down By Bombing" New York Post 8 October 1969: 1.

25. Seedman, 222.

26. "Bang? Boom!"

27. Alpert, "Profile" 34.

28. Dobbin.

29. Alpert, Growing 218-219.

30. Alpert, Growing 218.

31. Alpert, Growing 218-219.

32. Alpert, Growing 226.

33. Alpert, Growing 209-210.

34. Alpert, Growing 219-220.

Seedman, 220.

35. "Letter to Times on Bombing Here" New York Times 12 November 1969: 22.

36. *CBS* 11 November 1969 12:40

37. *ABC* 11 November 1969 23:20

38. J.Q. Rat, "All the Low Down on the Blow Down" Rat Subterranean News, 12-25 November, 1969: 3.

39. Larry Kleinman, "Probe Tips on the Bombings" New York Post 11 November, 1969: 1.

40. "Bombs Go Off at G.M. Building, Rockefeller Center, Chase Plaza" New York Times 11 November, 1969: 1.

41. Kleinman

42. "Bombs Go Off at G.M. Building, Rockefeller Center, Chase Plaza."

43. "Bombs Go Off at G.M. Building, Rockefeller Center, Chase Plaza."

44. Kleinman.

45. Kleinman.

46. Francis X. Clines "Bombs Here Linked to 4 Earlier Blasts; Letter Attacks War" New York Times 12 November, 1969: 1.

47. "Bombs Go Off at G.M. Building, Rockefeller Center, Chase Plaza."

48. Seedman, 227.

49. Kleinman.

50. Arthur Greenspan and Mike Pearl "The Bombings: Evidence Indicates It's One Man" New York Post, 12 November, 1969: 3.

51. Linda Greenhouse "Rash of Phone Threats Follow Blasts in Three Buildings Here" New York Times, 12 November, 1969:

NOTES

22.
52. Seedman, 227.

CHAPTER 4

1. Jane Alpert, Growing Up Underground (New York: William Morrow & Company,
1981) 225-227.
2. Alpert, Growing 220.
3. Albert A. Seedman and Peter Hellman, Chief! (New York: Arthur Fields Books, Inc., 1974) 236-237.
4. "Post Gets Letter on Court Bombing" New York Post 13 November 1969: 5.
5. Sundiata Acoli, "A Brief History of the Black Panther Party and It's Place in the Black Liberation Movement" The Talking Drum.com <http://www.thetalkingdrum.com/bla2.html>.
6. Seedman, 229-230.
7. Joseph B. Treaster, "Court Building Bombed: F.B.I. Seizes 2 at Armory" New York Times 13 November 1969: 1.
8. Alpert, Growing 227.
9. Lee Merrick, "Life With 'Crazy' George" RAT Subterranean News 12-25 November 1969: 10.
10. Jane Alpert, "Profile of Sam Melville" Letters From Attica by Samuel Melville (New York: William Morrow & Company, Inc., 1972) 28 & 35-37.
11. Seedman, 229.
12. Alpert, Growing 227.
13. Seedman, 230-232.
14. Seedman, 233. This source quotes two o'clock but every archived news source quotes four o'clock. Given the nature of the sources, four o'clock was chosen as most likely to be accurate.

CHAPTER 5

1. Albert A. Seedman and Peter Hellman, Chief! (New York: Arthur Fields Books, Inc., 1974) 226.
2. Seedman, 233-234.
3. Seedman, 233.
4. John Cohen, "Introduction" Letters From Attica by Samuel Melville (New York: William Morrow & Company, Inc., 1972)

52-55.

5. Jane Alpert, Growing Up Underground (New York: William Morrow and Company, Inc., 1981) 229. In this source, Alpert uses an alias to represent Dave Hughey. In the actual quote, the alias' last name was used in this source.

6. Alpert, Growing 228-230.

7. Cohen, 54-55.

8. Arthur Greenspan and Mike Pearl, "The Bombings: Evidence Indicates It's One Man" New York Post 12 November 1969: 3.

9. Alpert, Growing 230-231.

10. Media and law enforcement often claimed that the bombs were actually planted in the Army trucks before the arrests were made. In some cases they then go on to allege that the bombs were found on Sam's person, with no mention of inconsistency.

11. ABC 13 November 1969 21:50.

12. "Little Known of 5th Person in Case" New York Times 14 November 1969: 50.

13. Robert D. McFadden, "Sketches of 4 Seized as Bombing Suspects: Jane Lauren Alpert" New York Times 14 November 1969: 50.

14. Henry Raymont, "Sketches of 4 Seized as Bombing Suspects: John D. Hughey 3rd" New York Times 14 November 1969: 50.

15. Martin Arnold, "3 men and Woman Are Held in High Bail – Arrests Follow Surveillance" New York Times 14 November 1969: 1.

16. David Bird, "Sketches of 4 Seized as Bombing Suspects: Samuel Joseph Melville" New York Times 14 November 1969: 50.

17. Arnold.

18. Marvin Smilon and Sandor M. Polster, "Charge Four in Bombings" New York Post 13 November 1969: 1.

19. Arnold.

20. William E. Farrell, "Sketches of 4 Seized as Bombing Suspects: George Demmerle" New York Times 14 November 1969: 50.

21. Lee Merrick, "Life With 'Crazie' George" RAT Subterranean News 12-25 November 1969: 10.

22. Jerry Rubin, We Are Everywhere (New York: Harper & Row,

1971) 216-218.

23. "Robert DePugh and The Minutemen" The Nizkor Project Paranoia as Patriotism: Far Right Influences on the Militia Movement <http://www.nizkor.org/hweb/orgs/american/adl/ paranoia-as-patriotism/minutemen.html>.

24. Paul Simon, "Demmerle a Paid Informer Since '66" RAT Subterranean News, 7-20 January 1970: 4.

25. "George" RAT Subterranean News, 5 June 1970: 6-7.

26. Seedman, 238.

CHAPTER 6

1. Jeff Shiro, "Rat and the Bombings" RAT Subterranean News, 12-23 November 1969: 2.

2. "Sam Melville Denied Bail" RAT Subterranean News, 7-20 January 1970: 4.

3. Jane Alpert, "Profile of Sam Melville" Letters From Attica by Samuel Melville (New York: William Morrow & Company, Inc., 1972) 41.

4. Samuel Melville, "February 12, 1970, Dear Brother," Letters From Attica (New York: William Morrow & Company, Inc., 1972) 97.

5. Melville, "May 16, 1970, Dear Brother" 110-112.

6. Alpert, "Profile" 41.

7. Albert A. Seedman and Peter Hellman, Chief! (New York: Arthur Fields Books, Inc., 1974) 237.

8. Jane Alpert, Growing Up Underground (New York: William Morrow & Company, 1981) 244-247.

9. John Cohen, "Introduction" Letters From Attica by Samuel Melville (New York: William Morrow & Company, Inc., 1972) 79.

10. Alpert, "Profile" 42-43.

11. J.Q. Rat, "All the Low Down on the Blow Down" RAT Subterranean News 12-25 November 1969: 3.

12. Paul Simon, "Epilogue" RAT Subterranean News 12-25 November 1969: 26.

13. David Hughey, "David Hughey Speaks" RAT Subterranean News 12-25 November 1969: 3.

MAD BOMBER MELVILLE

CHAPTER 7

1. Samuel Melville, "November, 1969, My Dear Brother" Letters From Attica (New York: William Morrow & Company, Inc., 1972) 85-86.

2. Melville, "Tuesday, January 20, 1970, Dear Brother" 89.

3. Melville, "January 26, 1970, Dear Brother" 91.

4. Melville, "March, 1970, Prison Life – Light" 101.

5. Jane Alpert, "Profile of Sam Melville" Letters From Attica by Samuel Melville (New York: William Morrow & Company, Inc., 1972) 43.

6. Melville, "March, 1970, Dear Brother" 100-101.

7. Melville, "March 14, 1970, Lenny" 102.

8. Melville, "April 2, 1970, Ruth" 106-107.

9. Melville, "April 20, 1970, Dear Brother": 109.

10. Melville, "May 28, 1970, Dear Brother, 2 Days later" 113.

11. Melville, "May 16, 1970, Dear Brother" 110.

12. Melville, 114-118.

13. Melville, "August 10, 1970, Dear Brother" 122.

14. Melville, "Aug. 31, 1970, Dear Brother" 124.

15. John Cohen, "Introduction" Letters From Attica by Samuel Melville (New York: William Morrow & Company, Inc., 1972) 55-59.

CHAPTER 8

1. Samuel Melville Letters From Attica "September 6, 1970, Dear John" (New York: William Morrow & Company, 1981) 125.

2. Melville, "September 20, 1970" 126.

3. Coons, 197.

4. William R. Coons Attica Diary (New York: Stein and Day, 1972) 174-175.

5. Coons, 195-196.

6. Melville, "December 25, 1970" 129.

7. Melville, "January 30, 1971, Dear Bill" 133.

8. Melville, "December 25, 1970" 129.

9. Melville, "February 9, 1971, Dear Brother" 134.

10. Melville, "March 21, 1971, Dear Brother John" 138-139.

11. Melville, "April 18, 1971" 143.

12. Melville, "May 7, 1971, Dear People" 144-147.

NOTES

13. Melville, "Report" 149-150.

14. Melville, "History of the Attica Strike" 150-151.

15. John Cohen, "Introduction" Letters From Attica by Samuel Melville (New York: William Morrow & Company, Inc., 1972) 63.

16. Melville, "June 2, 1971" 155.

17. Melville, "June 4, 1971, Dear Bill" 155.

18. Melville, "May 19, 1971, Dear Bill" 154.

19. Melville, "July 2, 1971, Bill" 159.

20. Coons, 204.

21. Melville, "June 20, 1971" 157.

22. Melville, "May 18, 1971, Dear Swami" 153.

23. Melville, "June 5, 1971, Dear Brother" 155-156.

24. Melville, "July 1, 1971, Dear Brother" 157-158.

25. Melville, "The Iced Pig, Number 1" 161-162.

26. Melville, "July 27, 1971, Dear People" 162-163.

27. Melville, Footnote, 163.

28. Melville, "August 6, 1971, Dear People" 163-164.

29. Melville, "August 6, 1971, Dear People" 163-164.

30. Coons, 214.

31. Melville, "August 1971, Sister Harriet" 165-166.

32. Melville, "The Iced Pig, Number 2" 167-168.

33. Melville, "August 71, Poder Hermano!" 168-169.

34. Cohen, 66.

35. Cohen, 64.

36. Melville, "August 20, 1971, People" 168.

37. Melville, "The Iced Pig, Number 3" 170-171.

38. Joseph Martin, Nat Kantner, Donald Flynn, Alex Michrlini, Jean Perry and Donald Singleton "Attica, Anatomy of a Tragedy" Special New York Daily News Report 4-8 October 1971.

39. Melville, "August 30, 1971, Brother John" 172.

40. Melville, "August 30, 1971, Dear Bill" 171.

41. Melville, "July 27, 1971, Dear People" 162-163.

42. Melville, "April 1, 1971, My Oppressed Sister" 141.

43. Melville, "September 4, 1971" 173-174.

CHAPTER 9

1. Bob Buyer and Ray Hill, "Attica Inmates Seize Four Cellblocks:

11 Guards Hurt, Others Held Hostage" Buffalo Evening News 9 September 1971: 1.

2. Buyer, "Attica Inmates Seize Four Cellblocks…".

3. Bob Buyer, "Woman Fears for Inmate Husband as Attica Riot Erupts" Buffalo Evening News 9 September 1971: 1.

4. Bob Buyer, "Woman Fears…".

5. Cy Egan and William H. Rudy, "New Riot in Attica Cellblock" New York Post 10 September 1971: 1.

6. Paul MacClennan, Bob Buyer and Ray Hill, "Attica Inmates Demanding Amnesty; Hostages Still Held as Talks Bog Down" Buffalo Evening News 10 September 1971: 1.

7. Tom Wicker, A Time to Die (New York: Quadrangle, 1975) Appendix One.

8. "Now, Attica Again" New York Times 11 September 1971: 26.

9. Bob Buyer, "Prisoners Offer News Reporter a Portrait of Desperate Lives" Buffalo Evening News 10 September 1971: 1.

10. Jerry Allan, "State's Correction Aides Split Anew by Attica Riot: Rehabilitate or Get Tough?" Buffalo Evening News 10 September 1971: 8.

11. Allan.

12. Francis X. Clines, "Attica Has No Fear, but Anger Aplenty" New York Times 10 September 1971: 31.

13. Barbara Trecker, "50 Demonstrate Here for Prisoners" New York Post 10 September 1971: 21.

14. "Alarm Bell Tolls at Attica" Buffalo Evening News 10 September 1971: 40.

15. Buffalo Evening News Bureau, "Rocky Given Briefings, Doesn't Plan Attica Visit" Buffalo Evening News 10 September 1971: 9.

16. Paul MacClennan, "Reporter Finds World Inside Wall Grim, Unreal, Relatively Safe" Buffalo Evening News 11 September 1971: 7.

17. Bob Buyer, Paul MacClennan and Ray Hill, "Progress Reported in Attica Talks" Buffalo Evening News 11 September 1971: 1.

18. Paul MacClennan, "Hostages at Attica Tired, Tense but Well-Treated" Buffalo Evening News 11 September 1971: 1.

19. "Amnesty Question Discussed By Overseers, Wyoming DA"

NOTES

Buffalo Evening News 11 September 1971: 6.

20. "Time Bomb" cartoon, Buffalo Evening News 11 September 1971: B-2.

21. Linda Charlton, "Schoolteacher Turned Warden" New York Times 13 September 1971: 71.

22. Fred Ferretti, "Amnesty Demand Called Snag in Attica Prison Talks" New York Times 12 September 1971: 1.

23. Ferretti, "Amnesty Demand Called Sang in Attica Prison Talks".

24. Fred Ferretti, "Attica Prisoners Win 28 Demands, But Still Resist" New York Times 13 September 1971: 1.

25. Ferretti, "Attica Prisoners Win 28 Demands, But Still Resist".

26. "Rockefeller Bars a Visit to Attica" New York Times 13 September 1971: 71.

27. Ferretti, "Attica Prisoners Win 28 Demands, But Still Resist".

28. Ferretti, "Attica Prisoners Win 28 Demands, But Still Resist".

29. Paul MacClennan, Lee Coppola and Ray Hill, "Nine Hostages, 28 Prisoners Die in All-Out Attica Attack" Buffalo Evening News 13 September 1971: 1.

30. MacClennan, "Nine Hostages, 28 Prisoners Die in All-Out Attica Attack".

31. MacClennan, "Nine Hostages, 28 Prisoners Die in All-Out Attica Attack".

32. Fred Ferretti, "9 Hostages and 28 Prisoners Die as 1,000 Storm Prison in Attica; 28 Rescued, Scores are Injured" New York Times 14 September 1971: 1.

33. "Freed Hostages Go to Hospitals; One of Them Dies" Buffalo Evening News 13 September 1971: 1.

34. Jay Levin, "Battle of Attica: Death's Timetable" New York Post 14 September 1971: 3.

35. MacClennan, "Nine Hostages, 28 Prisoners Die in All-Out Attica Attack".

36. MacClennan, "Nine Hostages, 28 Prisoners Die in All-Out Attica Attack".

37. MacClennan, "Nine Hostages, 28 Prisoners Die in All-Out

Attica Attack".
38. "Freed Hostages Go to Hospitals."
39. Leonard Katz, "Nine Hostages, 28 Convicts Slain in Battle for Attica" New York Post 13 September 1971: 3.
40. "Militants Blamed by the Governor" New York Post 13 September 1971: 2.
41. "Militants Blamed by the Governor".
42. Ferretti, "9 Hostages and 28 Prisoners Die."
43. "Seale Blames Oswald for Deaths" Buffalo Evening News 13 September 1971: 1.
44. Fred Ferretti, "Convicts Revolt at Attica, Hold 32 Guards Hostage" New York Times 10 September 1971: 1.
45. Clines.
46. "Men From Harlem and Bed-Stuy Guarded by 'Farmers'" New York Times 12 September 1971: E-8.
47. McCandlish Phillips, "Despite Violence Within Prison Walls, Town of Attica Maintains an Air of Serenity" New York Times 14 September 1971: 28.
48. "Statement by Commissioner Oswald" New York Times 14 September 1971: 28.
49. Leonard Katz and Jay Levin, "Hostages Died of Gunshot Wounds" New York Post 14 September 1971: 1.
50. Lee Coppola, "Bloodstains, Litter – Reminders of Death, Violence Inside Attica" Buffalo Evening News 14 September 1971: 1.
51. "We Had Only a Week to Go" New York Post 18 September 1971: 3.
52. Joseph Lelyveld, "Findings Shock Families of Hostages" New York Times 15 September 1971: 1.

CHAPTER 10
1. John "Splitting the Sky" Boncore, personal interview with author, 26 September 2005.
2. Milton M. Klein, The Empire State: A History of New York State (Ithaca, NY: Cornell University Press, 2001) 689.
3. Michael M. Baden and Judith Adler Hennessee, Unnatural Death: Confessions of a Medical Examiner (New York: Random House, 1989) 196.

NOTES

4. John Cohen, "Introduction" <u>Letters From Attica</u> by Samuel Melville (New York: William Morrow & Company, Inc., 1972) 73.

5. Russell G. Oswald, <u>Attica – My Story</u> (Garden City, NY: Doubleday & Company, Inc., 1972) 23.

6. Oswald, 23-24.

7. Oswald, 263.

8. William Kunstler, Forward, <u>Letters From Attica</u> by Samuel Melville (New York: William Morrow & Company, Inc., 1972) vii-x.

9. <u>Attica; the Official Report of the New York State Special Commission on Attica</u> (USA: Bantam, September 1972) Appendix D.

10. Michael T. Kaufman, "Bomb-Carrying Convict Killed by Sharpshooter" <u>New York Times</u> 14 September 1971: 29.

11. "'Bomber' Dies" <u>Buffalo Evening News</u> 15 September 1971: Section I.

12. Robert E. Tomasson, "Melville, Attica Radical, Dead; Recently Wrote of Jail Terror" <u>New York Times</u> 15 September 1971: 34.

13. Brian B. King, "Attica Revisited After Nine Months" <u>Olean Times Herald</u> 5 June 1972: 4.

14. M. Wesley Swearingen, <u>F.B.I. Secrets: An Agent's Exposé</u> (Boston: South End Press, 1995) 65.

15. Jeremy Varon, <u>Bringing the War Home: the Weather Underground, the Red Army Faction, and Revolutionary Violence in the Sixties and Seventies</u> (Berkeley: University of California Press, 2004) 149.

16. Richard X Clark, <u>The Brothers of Attica: The Inmates' Spokesman Tells What Happened Inside the Prison During the Fateful Days of the Attica Rebellion</u> (New York: Links, 1973) 122.

17. <u>Attica</u> 397-398.

18. Annette T. Rubinstein, <u>Attica</u> (New York: The New York Charter Group for a Pledge of Conscience, 1975) 4.

19. <u>Life Magazine</u> 1 October 1971: 28.

20. John "Splitting the Sky" Boncore.

21. Liz Fink, personal interview with author, 16 January 2007.

22. Sharon Berman, personal interview with author, 20 September

2006.

23. Kunstler, "Forward" ix.

24. William M. Kunstler, "Ethics, the Law and the Body Politic" University at Buffalo School of Architecture and Planning commencement speech, May 13, 1995, CounterPunch 7 May 2003 <http://www.counterpunch.org/jackson05072003.html>.

25. "Albany Offices Bombed in Reprisal for Attica" Buffalo Evening News 18 September 1971: 7.

26. Cy Egan, "Blast Rocks Oswald Office" New York Post 18 September 1971: 3.

EPILOGUE

1. Jane Alpert, Growing Up Underground (New York: William Morrow & Company, 1981) 303-306.

2. "Jane Alpert's Bail in Bomb-Plot Case Declared Forfeited" New York Times 15 May 1970.

3. Lucinda Franks, "The 4-Year Odyssey of Jane Alpert, From Revolutionary Bomber to Feminist" New York Times 14 January 1975: 14.

"Underground Odyssey" Time 27 January 1975: 63.

4. Linda Charlton, "Memorial to a Radical Leader Written by a Fugitive" New York Times 1 March 1972: 79.

5. "Underground Odyssey" Time 27 January 1975: 63.

6. Lucinda Franks, "The 4-Year Odyssey of Jane Alpert, From Revolutionary Bomber to Feminist" New York Times 14 January 1975: 14.

7. Robert McG. Thomas Jr., "Jane Alpert Gives Up After Four Years" New York Times 15 November 1974: 1.

8. "Underground Odyssey" Time 27 January 1975: 63.

9. Lucinda Franks, "The 4-Year Odyssey of Jane Alpert, From Revolutionary Bomber to Feminist" New York Times 14 January 1975: 14.

10. Jane Alpert, "Mother Right: A New Feminist Theory" Documents From the Women's Liberation Movement: An On-Line Archival Collection Special Collections Library, Duke University <http://scriptorium.lib.duke.edu/wlm/mother/>.

11. Robert McG. Thomas Jr., "Jane Alpert Gives Up After Four Years" New York Times 15 November 1974: 1.

NOTES

12. "Jane Alpert Returns" New York Times 17 November 1974: 248.

13. Lucinda Franks, "Jane Alpert Says Surfacing Was 'the Right Thing to Do'" New York Times 16 November 1974: 18.

14. Arnold H. Lubasch, "Jane Alpert is Sentenced Here to 27 Months for Bombing Conspiracy and Jumping Bail in 1970" New York Times 14 January 1975: 15.

15. Robert McG. Thomas Jr., "Jane Alpert Gives Up After Four Years" New York Times 15 November 1974: 1.

16. "Fugitives: One Came Home" Newsweek 25 November 1974: 42.

17. *ABC* 1/27/75 5:06.

18. Robert McG. Thomas Jr., "Jane Alpert Gives Up After Four Years" New York Times 15 November 1974: 1.

19. Lucinda Franks, "Lawyer for Jane Alpert Denies She Informed on Other Radical Fugitives" New York Times 13 April 1975: 52.

20. Arnold H. Lubasch, "Jane Alpert Given Four-Month Term: Sentenced for Contempt – She Had Served 20 Months in Bomb Case" New York Times 7 October 1977: 28.

21. Liz Fink, personal interview with the author, 16 January 2007.

22. Deborah Larned, "Pat Swinton Acquitted" Sevendays 6 October 1975: 6.

23. Eden Ross Lipson, "A Bomber's Confessions" New York Times 25 October 1981: BR3

Index

INDEX

I

Iced Pig, The 89, 90, 114

J

Jackson, George 95, 96, 106, 110, 114, 116
Jackson, Jonathan 96
John Birch Society 57

K

Kunstler, William 108, 110, 116, 122

L

Le Petit Journal 14
Liberation News Service (LNS) 23

M

Magee, Ruchell 96
Mancusi, Vincent R. 83, 84, 93, 97, 100, 105, 106
Marine Midland Bank 19, 22, 58
Marine Midland Grace Trust 20, 21, 23
Marxists 6. See also communism
McCarthy, Joseph 3
McCurdy, David 15, 42
Metesky, George 8
Midnight Special 129
Milwaukee Federal building 86
Minuteman 58
Moby Dick 3, 6, 122
Ms. Magazine 127

N

National Guard Armory 68th Regiment 45
National Mobilization Against the War 34
New York Police Department 30, 39
New York Post 20, 28, 51, 52
New York Times 5, 28, 53, 54, 106, 107, 117, 128, 131
Nixon, Richard 26, 27, 33
North American Congress on Latin America 6, 21, 53

O

Oswald, Russell 87, 100
Oughton, Diana 65

P

Palmer, Robin 118, 121, 122
Panther 13, 43, 56, 65
Peace and Freedom Party 5
Pyronics, Inc. 17

Q

Quinn, William 100, 105, 106

R

Ramparts 88
RAT Subterranean News 6, 11, 18, 23, 24, 30, 32, 53, 62, 63, 66
RCA building 36, 38
Robbins, Terry 65
Robeson, Paul 3
Roche, James 35
Rockefeller, David 35, 38
Rubin, Jerry 56

S

Sam Melville Collective 15-19, 22, 23, 30, 32-34, 42, 66, 69
Saxe, Susan 130
Seale, Bobby 107, 110
Selective Service 27, 32
Sing Sing 75, 76
Soledad Brother 96
Standard Oil 21, 35, 36-39, 43, 51, 52
Students for a Democratic Society 6, 44
Student Nonviolent Coordinating Committee 34
Sullivan, Joseph 80
Swinton, Pat 6, 16, 34, 42, 52, 86, 129, 130

T

Time magazine 126
Tombs, The 74-76, 116

INDEX

U

U.S. Army 17, 27, 30, 31, 131
United Fruit Company 16, 17, 131
University of Wisconsin 35

V

Vallières, Pierre 8
Vietnam War 5, 6, 26, 32, 34-36, 53, 118, 121, 128
Villeneuve, Raymond 9

W

W.R. Grace & Co 19, 21
Weathermen 44, 56, 65, 66, 68, 88, 126
Whitehall Induction Center 31, 32-34, 43, 51, 66
White Niggers of America 9
Wilkerson, Cathy 65
Wood, Lee 75
Woodstock Music and Art Festival 16

Y

Yippies 44, 56, 57

Leslie James Pickering was a Founder and Spokesperson for the North American Earth Liberation Front Press Office, serving with the organization from early 2000 until the summer of 2002. During this period the Press Office sustained two raids by the Federal Bureau of Investigation, the Bureau of Alcohol Tobacco and Firearms and local law enforcement agencies, responded to over a half dozen grand jury subpoenas, conducted public presentations, produced booklets, newspapers, magazines, and a video on the Earth Liberation Front and handled the public release of communiqués for dozens of the most vital Earth Liberation Front actions.

Through the Press Office, Leslie was the editor of *Resistance, the Journal of the North American Earth Liberation Front Press Office*, and many other independently produced materials regarding the Earth Liberation Front. Leslie has handled countless local, national and international media inquires, resulting in articles in *The New York Times, The Washington Times, The Los Angeles Times, USA Today, Christian Science Monitor, Rolling Stone, The Village Voice* and many more, conducted interviews with ABC, NBC, CNN, FOX, CBC, BBC, National Geographic TV and many others, and has given lectures at American University, Lewis & Clark College, Saint Michael's University, Furman University, Bard College, New York University, Fresno State College, Macalester College, University of West Los Angeles, Princeton University,

Mercyhurst College, Syracuse University, Buffalo State College and others.

Leslie's first book, *Earth Liberation Front 1997-2002* was published by Arissa Media Group in 2003 and he has written articles in the *Earth First! Journal* and *Igniting a Revolution: Voices in Defense of the Earth* published on AK Press and others. He has a California High School Equivalency Diploma, a BA in Community Organizing and Journalism and a MA in History of American Social Justice Struggles and Journalism from Goddard College. Leslie lives in his hometown of Buffalo, NY.

ALSO AVAILABLE FROM ARISSA MEDIA GROUP

EARTH LIBERATION FRONT 1997-2002
Leslie James Pickering

The first book to be published on the underground Earth Liberation Front, tracing its first five years of activity through communiques, underground newspapers, interviews and news releases. Edited by former ELF spokesperson Leslie James Pickering.

256pp. ISBN 0974288403 pbk.

SOCIAL CRISIS AND SOCIAL DEMORALIZATION
The Dynamics of Status in American Race Relations
Ronald Kuykendall

This alternative perspective on the problem of American race relations takes sharp aim at issues of status, power and political class. In his insightful exploration, political scientist Ronald Kuykendall argues that the racial problem is a political class conflict that must be resolved through revolutonary political class struggle. He adeptly unravels the complex interrelationships of status, political repression, and social stratification involved in American race issues. As the social crisis of race relations threatens to boil over in 21st century America, the content of this book is critical. Looking at the roots of the "race problem" as a power dynamic, what solutions - if any - seem possible? Can this crisis be resolved?

128pp. ISBN 0974288438 pbk.

THE LOGIC OF POLITICAL VIOLENCE
Lessons in Reform and Revolution
Craig Rosebraugh

Within westernized societies, particularly the United States, there has been a near universal acceptance that nonviolent action has been the foundation on which the progress and success of social justice movements has been built. Yet, contrary to popular beliefs held by many in the United States, political violence has played a crucial role in advancing historical justice struggles.

In this breakthrough study, Rosebraugh examines the historical roles that both nonviolence and political violence have played in social and political movements both in the United States and internationally. His profound and well researched conclusions advocate for the necessity of a political and social revolution in the United States using any means necessary.

The Logic of Political Violence is an excellent resource for those contemplating political and social change in the United States. It is a must-read for everyone involved in US political and social movements, especially for those wondering why single issue pursuits rarely, if ever, are ultimately successful. Challenging the predominant societal norms on the political and social change process in the United States, Rosebraugh has made an important contribution to the struggle that may very well become the new American Revolution.

288pp. ISBN 0974288411 pbk.

THE LOGIC OF POLITICAL VIOLENCE
Craig Rosebraugh Live at Laughing Horse Books
Spoken Word CD

This lecture examines the historic roles that political violence and nonviolence have played in social and political movements in the United States and internationally. A 65-minute spoken word cd recorded live at Laughing Horse Books in Portland, Oregon on January 10, 2003.

arissa
media group